EQUAL PAY FOR WORK OF EQUAL VALUE

Also by Michael Rubenstein

A PRACTICAL GUIDE TO THE EMPLOYMENT PROTECTION ACT

UNFAIR DISMISSAL: A Guide to the Relevant Case Law (*with Yvonne Frost*)

EQUAL PAY FOR WORK OF EQUAL VALUE

The New Regulations and their Implications

Michael Rubenstein
Editor, Industrial Relations Law Reports

M

First published 1984 by
THE MACMILLAN PRESS LTD
London and Basingstoke
Companies and representatives
throughout the world

Printed in Great Britain by
Camelot Press Ltd
Southampton

Typeset by
Wessex Typesetters Ltd
Frome, Somerset

British Library Cataloguing in Publication Data
Rubenstein, Michael
Equal pay for work of equal value
1. Great Britain—Equal pay (Amendment) Regulations 1983 2. Wages—Women—Law and legislation—Great Britain
3. Equal pay for equal work—Law and legislation—Great Britain
I. Title
344.104'1421 KD3103.W6
ISBN 0–333–37557–2

To Bar, my wife, and to Shirley, my mother, for their support and inspiration

Contents

1 Introduction

Equal pay for work of equal value has been a slogan of the women's movement for generations. On 1 January 1984, amidst confusion and controversy, it became a legal right in Britain.

This book attempts to explain the Equal Pay (Amendment) Regulations 1983: how they can be used by applicants, how they may affect employers, how they may be interpreted by the courts. It does so by placing equal pay for work of equal value in the context of discrimination law generally. Although the new Regulations were enacted in order to comply with the declaration of the European Court of Justice that the United Kingdom was in breach of European Community law, equal pay for work of equal value has long been regarded by many as the next logical step in the development of a legal framework to deal with women's disadvantaged economic status.

The Equal Pay Act 1970 prohibited the most blatant forms of pay discrimination – unequal pay for the same or broadly similar work, unequal pay for work rated as equivalent by the employer's evaluation scheme, and separate 'women's rates' in collective agreements. In the immediate aftermath of the Act, the differential between the sexes was narrowed but since 1977 it has remained relatively stable. In 1982, according to the New Earnings Survey, women's full-time hourly earnings were 73.9 per cent of men's. At the same time, applications brought under the Act had decreased from 1742 in 1976, the first year the statute was in force, to thirty-nine in 1982.

In Chapter 2, we look at the main reasons why women continue to receive lower pay than men. This chapter emphasises the importance of occupational and job segregation by sex. Most women are employed on 'women's work' and most men do 'men's jobs' (I use these terms throughout as a convenient descriptive shorthand and not in a sexist sense). This means that there was an in-built limitation on the extent to which the Equal Pay Act could reduce differentials since, for large numbers of women, there has been no male comparator employed on like work.

In the long term, it is generally agreed that the answer to job segregation is to ensure equality of opportunity. This is the aim of the Sex Discrimination Act 1975, which prohibits discrimination on grounds of sex in recruitment, training and promotion. The aspirations of the Sex Discrimination Act, for the most part, however, remain just that. There is no evidence that the 1975 Act has resulted in any marked decrease in job segregation by sex. In any event, the remedies which the Sex Discrimination Act provides are more likely to be of use to new entrants to the labour market rather than to women who have worked in segregated employment for many years. Women who have invested in training to become a nurse, for example, are unlikely in mid-career to apply for jobs as truck drivers merely because the law now prohibits exclusion from that job on grounds of sex.

Thus, the Equal Pay Act and the Sex Discrimination Act produced an anomaly in that the women who had suffered most from discrimination – those employed in segregated women's jobs – stood to gain the least from the legislation. This is where the new right to equal pay for work of equal value fits in. For the first time, women in segregated employment have the opportunity, albeit a limited one, to complain that their pay has been discriminatorily depressed.[1]

The significance of this in the context of the wage gap between the sexes is discussed in Chapter 2. That chapter points out that there are a variety of causes for women's lower pay, that some of the reasons are not susceptible to legal solutions and that there is no single legal solution to which the problem is susceptible. Women, on average, have less productivity-enhancing characteristics than men. This results in part from free choice, in part from 'socialisation' about women's role, in part from the division of labour within the family and in part from discrimination in education and pre-employment training. These explanations of the pay differential between men and women are all exogenous to discrimination by a given employer.

Nonetheless, differences in personal attributes explain only a small part of the pay gap. Where men and women have equal productivity characteristics, women are still paid substantially less than men. The key to explaining the bulk of the differential lies in the different jobs held by women and men. Why should this result in differences of pay? One explanation is that the jobs which women do are less productive or 'valuable' than those done by men, notwithstanding that the women are equally capable of doing the more productive jobs. This can be because women are forced into low-paying less productive work by discrimination; or it can be because women freely choose such jobs since they offer non-pecuniary advantages such as flexibility. To the extent that women are directed into jobs which are low paying and which would not pay any more if they were performed by men, the issue is one of employment discrimination, falling within the purview of the Sex Discrimination Act.

There is an alternative explanation, however, for the wage gap between equally qualified men and women. This is that the jobs which women do are equally productive or 'valuable' as the work done by men, but that the women's jobs are paid less because they are performed by women. Until now, there has been no legal remedy for the woman whose work was low paid because her job was mainly performed by women. The new Regulations provide such a remedy, albeit only where the woman is employed on work of equal value to that of a man in the same employment. In Chapter 2, we set out some of the arguments to support the view that women's work may be discriminatorily undervalued on grounds of sex. It is important to note here that though the arguments may be compelling as a matter of logic, there is really little direct evidence that women are paid less because they perform women's work. It is impossible to disentangle the relative contribution of employment discrimination and pay discrimination to determine the extent to which women are low paid because they are employed in low-paying jobs and the extent to which the jobs are low paying because they are dominated by women. Aside from anecdotal evidence, such research as is available is almost always on a 'macro' rather than an individual firm basis and, in any event, discrimination is estimated by an unexplained residual after all other factors have been accounted for, rather than directly.

This means that the diagnosis of the problem which the Regulations aim to cure is somewhat debatable. Even more controversial is the cure prescribed. The Regulations equate 'value' with the demands made by the job. Work of equal value is defined, in effect, as work which is equally demanding in terms of its job content. It is quite a leap, however, from finding that jobs have comparable content to the conclusion that they are of equal value to a given employer. Moreover, it is at least questionable whether 'value' can be separated in a meaningful way from the market. Water, as Adam Smith pointed out, has more use than diamonds but does not command the same price.

Thus, the issues posed by the concept of equal pay for work of equal value are exceedingly complex. They are qualitatively different from a like work case, because where workers are employed on similar work it can be reasonably assumed that they are interchangeable, whereas the new Regulations permit a claim to be brought requiring an assessment of the worth of jobs which have completely different characteristics. In such circumstances, we would have anticipated lengthy debate on the fundamental problems which must be resolved: questions such as how 'value' is to be determined, the role of the labour market in determining value, the criteria for comparing blue and white collar jobs, the difficulties in arriving at consistent evaluations, the standard for determining when an evaluation should be regarded as discriminatory, the impact of successful claims on collective agreements and grading schemes. Instead, the Goverment regarded itself as under pressure from the European Court to legislate quickly and, as we point out in Chapter 3, the procedure adopted for introducing the new law offered the minimum opportunity for debate and consideration.

One consequence is that the Regulations are drafted in language which, in places, borders on the incoherent. Lord Denning put the point well in the House of Lords debate:

'Ordinary individuals who are affected by equal pay for work of equal value ought to be able to read and understand the Regulations. Not one of them would be able to do so. No ordinary lawyer would be able to understand them. The Industrial Tribunals would have the greatest difficulty and the Court of Appeal would probably be divided in opinion.'[2]

It is my job to help you to understand what the new Regulations say, what they mean and what are their implications. Clearly, though, our chances of so doing successfully are circumscribed by the drafting of the Regulations. The Amendment Regulations and the Procedural Regulations which accompany them reach a new low in terms of lack of clarity, exceeding such previous exemplars of obscure draftsmanship as the Transfer of Undertakings Regulations and the sections of the Employment Act on secondary industrial action. In those earlier examples, the draftsman at least had the excuse that he was striving to come to terms with delicate nuances on complex problems. It might be thought that this could explain the lack of clarity in the equal value Regulations which, as we noted above, also pose difficult conceptual problems. Yet this is not what has happened. The complex issues, for the most part, have been circumvented by over-simplification and the really murky drafting relates to questions such as when an applicant should be permitted to bring a claim and how the report of the independent expert can be challenged. There is no valid reason why the rules for determining such relatively straightforward questions could not have been put in language that could be understood by the ordinary men and women at whom they are directed. That they have not suggests an uncertain grasp of the issues involved by those responsible for drafting the Regulations, or a lack of drafting competence, or an unconscionable disregard for the consequences of obscure language. Whichever is the real explanation, it must be a cause for serious concern.

The Regulations amend the Equal Pay Act 1970 by providing a presumptive right to equal pay 'where a woman is employed on work which . . . is, in terms of the demands made on her (for instance under such headings as effort, skill and decision), of equal value to that of a man in the same employment'. In Chapter 4, we look at the wide scope of claims that can be brought under the Regulations. Claims can be made across the existing boundaries of bargaining units, grading systems or job evaluation schemes. A woman clerical worker can claim that she is employed on work of equal value with a male manual worker and vice versa. Because the Equal Pay Act relates to all contractual terms and conditions (except pensions), an equal value claim does not have to be a claim for equal pay. It can relate to unequal treatment with regard to a non-wage contractual term or condition, such as sick pay benefits or subsidised mortgage schemes. We suggest that there is nothing to prevent an applicant making comparisons at the same time with a number of more highly paid men doing different kinds of work, and that in most circumstances it would make sense for a complainant so to do.

The procedural aspects of bringing a claim are considered in Chapter 5. The most significant relates to the preliminary screening hearing at which the Industrial Tribunal has to decide whether the complaint should be dismissed without further investigation. It will do this if it reaches the conclusion that there are 'no reasonable grounds for determining that the work is of equal value'.

One circumstance, according to the Regulations, in which a Tribunal must conclude that there are no reasonable grounds for determining that the work is of equal value is where the jobs in question have previously been evaluated as unequal under the employer's evaluation scheme and there are not reasonable grounds for determining that the employer's evaluation was discriminatory. Discriminatory job evaluation, treated as a peripheral issue under the Regulations but a central question for personnel and industrial relations practice, is the subject of Chapter 6. Here, we assess the kinds of job evaluation schemes which may be effective in blocking an equal value claim and conclude that non-analytic schemes are unlikely to suffice. We consider the bizarre test for whether a scheme discriminates as set out in the Regulations, a test which embodies no explicit standard of discrimination and determines whether an evaluation is discriminatory merely according to whether the Tribunal thinks its results are or are not 'justifiable'. We predict that applicants, nonetheless, will be expected to show evidence that the job evaluation has discriminated on grounds of sex either in intent or in effect. Using the principles of discrimination law developed under the Sex Discrimination, Race Relations and Equal Pay Acts, we suggest what this might entail. Our principal conclusion is that where jobs are segregated by sex so that women's work has different characteristics than that of men, any given choice of compensable factors or factor weightings may adversely impact upon women (or, if not, upon men). Whether such an outcome is 'justifiable', we suggest, is likely to be approached by tribunals on the basis that 'justifiable' will be equated with an outcome that is outside the band of reasonableness. Although at first sight harsh on the complainant, such a test would still offer ample scope for an applicant where an important aspect of her work was not taken into account in determining the compensable factors.

If an equal value claim is not blocked at the screening hearing, before it is referred to an independent expert the employer has an opportunity to contend that, in any event, the variation in pay was 'genuinely due to a material factor which is not the difference of sex'. If that defence is not raised at this stage, or if it does not succeed, the claim will go forward to investigation by an independent expert. The expert's role and his report is examined in Chapter 7. Of the most significance here are the parts of the Procedural Regulations setting out the grounds on which the expert's reasoning and conclusions may be challenged and the way in which this can be done. Each party is permitted to cross-examine the expert and to call their own expert witness, with a view to persuading the Tribunal, among other matters, that the expert reached a perverse conclusion. Despite a marked lack of clarity in the Regulations, it would appear that the Industrial Tribunal will make the ultimate determination as to whether the jobs being compared are of equal value and that it can reach a conclusion contrary to that of the independent expert without commissioning a new report.

If the Tribunal concludes that the work is not of equal value, that is the end of the claim. If the work is adjudged to be of equal value, the employer still has the opportunity to show that the variation in pay was due to a material factor other than the sex of the workers concerned. As a result of the decisions of the European Court and the EAT in the *Jenkins* v. *Kingsgate* cases,[3] it should be assumed that a defence to an equal value claim will not succeed not just where there is intentional discrimination, but also where the variation in pay is based on a factor which unjustifiably indirectly discriminates against women. There is one important difference between the employer's defence under the new Regulations and the defence to like work and work rated as equivalent claims. Whereas the material factor defence to a like work or equivalent work claim must be based on a material difference between the woman's case and the man's case, the defence to an equal value claim does not have to be so founded. This is the Government's response to the decision of the Court of Appeal in the *Clay Cross* case[4] that for there to be a material difference between the man's case and the woman's case, the difference must be based on the 'personal equation' of the workers concerned and not due to 'extrinsic forces'. In the *Clay Cross* case, 'market forces' were held to be extrinsic and therefore not a permissible ground for a variation in pay. The change in the wording is intended to permit labour market factors to justify a differential, at least in some circumstances. We suggest that it would be an over-simplification to interpret the law as never permitting market forces to be used. Likewise, it would be an over-simplification if market forces were regarded as a conclusive defence. Distinctions need to be drawn. One distinction is between cases where the complainant is a member of a group largely segregated by sex and cases where the work group concerned is relatively integrated. In the latter case, market forces should be regarded as permissible because their use is not sexually discriminatory. There are also important distinctions in the ways in which 'market forces' can have an impact on wage determination. Higher pay for a man because there is a genuine skill shortage for employees doing his kind of work and there is no such shortage of staff doing the woman's job may be regarded as an acceptable defence, provided it is proven by evidence. Lower pay for women because the employer can get them to work for less should not be regarded as acceptable and, if it is so treated, it is likely to conflict with European Community law. Other defences will also have to be judged by the standard of whether they discriminate in intent or in effect. The more prominent issues which will arise are also discussed in Chapter 8.

The role played by trade unions will be of considerable importance in determining the effectiveness of the Regulations. The substantive and procedural complexities of the Regulations are such that it seems all but impossible for an unrepresented litigant to conduct a case effectively. Trade unions are perfectly placed to provide the industrial expertise needed to ensure that their members are adequately represented. Historically, there has often been a large gap between official union policy on discrimination against women and union practice. However, with women's increased participation in the labour force, there are definite signs that this is changing. Nonetheless, equal pay for work of equal value will pose sensitive issues for the trade union movement. Claims under the Regulations will frequently involve conflicts of interest within particular trade unions and between different unions. Unions will have to choose between defending the status quo they themselves may have negotiated and representing their women members seeking to challenge existing differentials. These problems will not be easy to resolve.

What impact will the new Regulations have? One result that is certain is that they will not eliminate the wage gap between men and women. No law directed at arbitrary discrimination on grounds of sex can ever do that because some of the differential is for reasons which are neither arbitrary nor discriminatory. The objectives of eliminating sex-based discrimination in pay and that of achieving equality of pay between the sexes are by no means the same. To point to the continued existence of differentials after implementation of equal pay for work of equal value as conclusive proof that the legislation has not worked would be either naïve or mischievous.

Much of the impact of the new Regulations will depend upon how they are interpreted by Industrial Tribunals and the courts. As this manuscript was being completed, preliminary hearings in the first cases under the Regulations were taking place. There is an understandable strain of pessimism among feminists that little can be accomplished through legislation, and experience under other discrimination statutes suggests that the success or failure of the earliest cases (and the attendant publicity) will have a disproportionate impact on the number of claims that are ultimately brought. Particularly if women lose the initial cases, it will reinforce the widely held view that there is no point in trying to seek recourse against pay discrimination by using the law.

This would seriously constrain the effectiveness of the Regulations. For not only will the outcome of cases determine the number of complaints; the more claims that are brought, the more likely it is that they will succeed. The reasoning to support this proposition relates to the composition of the tribunals and the courts. Case law suggests that many judges are not entirely comfortable with concepts of discrimination law. Given their background and experience, this is not really surprising. With respect, the judges need educating. They need to understand that sex (and race) discrimination is not an aberration from the traditional English standard of fair play, but that discrimination is commonly subtle and systemic. The only effective way of 'educating' the judges is by bringing sufficient cases before them.[5] It is submitted that the more cases that are heard, the more the law is likely to be interpreted in accordance with its underlying objectives.

There is a second reason why the impact of the legislation will depend on the number of cases that are brought. It lies in the behaviour of employers. The dominant managerial imperative, so far as employment legislation is concerned, is to keep out of trouble. For these purposes at least, the average employer is an amoral pragmatist. If experience of dealing with personnel managers of all varieties over twenty years has taught me anything, it is that issues are not dealt with until they become a problem and when they become a problem they are dealt with. And nothing focuses the mind like an originating application from an Industrial Tribunal. A complaint, whether or not it is ultimately successful, requires the employer to justify what he has done. This, in itself, ensures that some attention is given to the problem. If cases are not brought, the Regulations will lose their credibility and other problems will take priority. If sufficient cases are brought, keeping the organisation out of trouble under the Regulations will become a personnel manager's priority. They will be more responsive to claims for less discriminatory pay structures. They will follow the case law to see what they need to do. They will take voluntary steps to avoid possible litigation and to comply with the new law.

From the standpoint of the employer, perhaps the most immediate voluntary steps to consider relate to job evaluation. Existing evaluation schemes should be reviewed to make some assessment as to whether they are likely to be regarded as discriminatory. Where work has not been evaluated, vulnerabilities under the Regulations should be determined and consideration given to whether job evaluation should be introduced. There are few advantages, and many disadvantages, to leaving the initial consideration of whether two jobs are of equal value to a Tribunal-appointed independent expert.

Where jobs might reasonably be considered to be of equal value, employers should review any pay differentials which exist to assess whether they are likely to be defendable.

In the long term, there is only one certain way for an employer to avoid the disruptive effects of a successful claim for equal pay for work of equal value. That is to ensure that women are not over-represented in particular jobs and under-represented in others.

NOTES

1. This is the answer to American writers such as Nelson, Opton and Wilson ('Wage Discrimination and the "Comparable Worth" Theory in Perspective', *University of Michigan Journal of Law Reform* vol. 13, no. 2, Winter 1980) who have argued that equal pay for work of equal value is a retrograde step towards achieving equal opportunity, since it may 'quash perhaps the most powerful incentive for women to enter occupations historically held by men: the prospect of higher pay'. Of course, the new Regulations do not offer a remedy to women whose work is *undervalued* on grounds of sex but who are not employed on work of *equal* value to that of any man.
2. *Hansard*, House of Lords, 5.12.83, col. 901.
3. *Jenkins* v. *Kingsgate (Clothing Productions) Ltd* [1981] IRLR 228 ECJ

and *Jenkins* v. *Kingsgate (Clothing Productions) Ltd No. 2* [1981] IRLR 388 EAT.

4. *Fletcher* v. *Clay Cross (Quarry Services) Ltd* [1978] IRLR 361 CA.
5. Anyone reading the decisions of Lord Denning in this field can see this process at work. Contrast, for example, the old-fashioned views expressed in *Automotive Products Ltd* v. *Peake* [1977] IRLR 365 CA on 'chivalry and courtesy which we expect mankind to give womankind' with the understanding of the problem shown, following wide-ranging submissions from counsel, in *E Coombes (Holdings) Ltd* v. *Shields* [1978] IRLR 263 CA or *Fletcher* v. *Clay Cross (Quarry Services) Ltd* [1978] IRLR 361 CA.

2 Why Women Are Paid Less Than Men

Women are paid less than men partly because of the attributes they bring to the job, partly because of the jobs they are in and partly because they are women. Discrimination may explain part of the wage gap between the sexes, but it certainly does not explain all of it. In the absence of discrimination by employers, average women's pay would not equal average men's pay. Personal characteristics which might be expected to lead to differences in productivity are an important explanation, but women with the same experience, qualifications and education as men earn substantially less. Occupational segregation is a major cause of the earnings differential, but the extent to which women choose to do 'women's work' is unclear. Some women doing women's work are paid less because, although they are equally productive as men, they have been placed in less productive jobs. Some women have been placed in jobs of equal value with men, but are paid less because they are women. Thus, there is no single answer to why women are paid less than men and it follows that there is no single solution which will result in that differential being eliminated.

This chapter looks at the explanations which have been proposed to account for the difference in earnings between men and women.

HUMAN CAPITAL DIFFERENCES

One approach attempts to explain differences in pay on the basis of differences between workers in personal characteristics or 'human capital', which are believed to affect productivity. We would expect that pay would vary according to the value of an employee's economic contribution to the firm. Because it is often impossible to measure individual productivity, an assumption is made that productivity will differ in accordance with differences in 'human capital' – such as education, work experience, training, continuity of work history – which are likely to determine an individual's productive capacity. All things being equal, we would expect two workers with the same experience, qualifications, training, and so on to be earning roughly the same wage. To the extent that men and women differ on average in types and levels of characteristics which are valued by employers as indicators of potential productivity, they will be selected for different jobs and paid different wages. It also follows that wage differences not accounted for by differences in productivity must be ascribed to other causes, including discrimination.

That there are important differences on average between men and women with respect to most productivity-related characteristics is beyond dispute. Thus, there are differences in educational qualifications obtained prior to entry into the labour force. In 1980, only 4 per cent of economically active women had degrees compared with 9 per cent of men. Twenty-four per cent of men had attained qualifications of GCE 'A' level or higher compared with 14 per cent of women and the proportion of men with 'O' level qualifications or better was 36 per cent compared with 26 per cent for women.[1] There are also marked differences according to sex in courses taken and areas of specialisation, with women being heavily represented in education and the more general cultural fields and poorly represented in disciplines with a strong vocational emphasis.[2]

Although differences in formal educational qualifications doubtless contribute to the earnings gap,[3] research suggests that they explain very little of the differential – of the order of 2 per cent according to one American study.[4] At all educational qualification levels, women's earnings are appreciably lower than those of men with the same level of qualification.[5] Thus, in 1980, median earnings for women with 'O' levels was 62 per cent of that of men with the same qualification.[6] These earnings figures have not been standardised for job experience, however, and it is to this that we must turn for a further explanation of the differential.

Simply as a function of the large increase in recent years in women's labour force participation, women's average experience has declined relative to that of men. In the United States, this has been put forward as an important explanation for the actual increase in the earnings differential between the sexes that has taken place in America over the past twenty years.[7] But the most significant cause of differences in experience stems from women's child-bearing and family responsibilities. As a result of this, women on average spend proportionately fewer years in the labour force than men. Their average length of service is shorter than that of men and they have a higher average turnover.[8] Therefore, women acquire less experience than men. Proponents of human capital theory assert that the result is that women acquire less productivity-enhancing, on-the-job training[9] and that these differences in work history are a major explanation for the difference in wages. The extent to which differences in experience result in lower productivity and its effect on wages is a subject of some controversy. In perhaps the best known human capital study, Mincer and Polachek, using American data, concluded that 45 per cent of the gap between the wages of men and women was explained by the duration of work experience.[10] On the other hand, it has been pointed out that years of service with the current employer appears to explain a great deal more of the differential than years of work experience generally, and it has been argued that the observed correlation between earnings and experience may simply be a reflection of higher pay resulting from seniority (including the effect of service payments under incremental pay systems) rather than differences in levels of productivity.[11]

How big a part, then, do average differences in personal characteristics play in the differential in pay? After a review of the literature, the prestigious US National Academy of Science's National Research Council concluded that 'worker characteristics account for very little of the difference in earnings; in fact, only two of the studies can explain more than 1/5th of the difference between men's and women's average earnings in terms of differences in worker characteristics'.[12]

Human capital economists argue that the differential remaining after adjustment could be further reduced if it were possible to control fully for differences in personal characteristics. Thus, economists employing human capital theory normally use years of schooling to measure the extent of an individual's education, but this makes no allowance for qualitative differences or for differences in job relevance.[13] Skills and abilities are never directly measured. Age has often been used as a proxy for experience where there are data limitations. More importantly, perhaps, there are important characteristics which are impossible to measure with any accuracy on a national, industrial or occupational level and for this reason are usually omitted. Job performance is a good example. Phelps Brown suggests that a major reason for so large a part of the variance in pay between the sexes remaining unexplained may be that 'the independent variables do not include the character traits that common observation suggests as being closely linked with economic advancement'.[14] Commitment to work is often cited as an important differentiating factor which is not easily measured, and it has been suggested that higher earnings for married men for given characteristics reflects their higher levels of motivation induced by family responsibilities, rather than discrimination in their favour.[15] By reasoning such as this, the unexplained wage gap can be regarded as an overestimate of the importance of discrimination.

Conversely, however, it can be argued that the limitations of human capital theory suggest that differences in wages ascribed to personal characteristics underestimate the role of discrimination. Thus, human capital theory does not resolve the key issue of cause and effect: that is, the extent to which low wages and discrimination discourage women from investing in human capital, the low investment in human capital in turn perpetuating women's lower earnings. Education differences, for example, between men and women in part may be the result, rather than the cause, of differences in employment opportunities.[16] Similarly, although women on average stay with the same employer for shorter periods than do men, the reasons for this higher turnover are debatable and are arguably at least partly a function of the kinds of jobs in which women are employed. It has been questioned whether a woman is more likely to leave a particular job than a similarly placed man.[17] That people will alter their behaviour in accordance with the way in which they are rewarded is well-documented.[18] To the extent that there is a 'feedback' effect, it casts doubt on the meaningfulness of estimating pay discrimination through adjusting for differences in human capital. Women's lower earnings in part result from their higher turnover and lack of continuous job experience, in line with the predictions of human capital theory. But women's higher turnover and discontinuous participation in the labour force are also the result of their lower earnings and the jobs in which they are employed. That is why women have been depicted as being trapped within a 'vicious circle'.

For these reasons, we may conclude that differences in personal characteristics, such as experience and education, leave a substantial part of the earnings gap between men and women unexplained.[19] Women, on average, earn substantially less than equally qualified men. This is not surprising, because until now we have not directly taken into account one of the most obvious differences between men and women: the jobs in which they are employed.

If equally qualified women earn less than equally qualified men, there are three principal possible explanations: first, that the equally qualified women are paid less because they have been discriminatorily assigned to jobs of less value because the jobs are less productive than those performed by men; second, that the women have chosen, despite their equal qualifications, to work in low-paid jobs because such work offers compensating non-pecuniary advantages; third, that the jobs performed by women and men are of equal value, but the employer is discriminating by paying the women less because they are women than he would pay if the same jobs were performed by men. In the remainder of this chapter, we look at each of these possibilities.

JOB SEGREGATION

Most women work in 'women's jobs' and most men work in 'men's jobs'. Jobs are substantially segregated by sex and there are substantial differences in earnings between occupations. Therefore, a second explanation for the pay differential between the sexes focuses on the jobs which men and women hold.

Most women in Britain work in female-dominated occupations. Hakim's study found that in 1971, although women only formed 36.5 per cent of the total labour force, 51 per cent of women worked in occupations which had 70 per cent or more women workers, a common touchstone for a segregated occupation.[20] Seventy-seven per cent of men worked in occupations which had 70 per cent or more male workers and a majority of men (53 per cent) worked in occupations with 90 per cent or more male workers. Therefore, women's under-representation in typically male jobs was even more marked than women's concentration in typically female jobs. The concentration of women into women's work appears to be increasing. Over two-thirds of working women in Britain are now employed in non-manual occupations compared with about one-third of men. About 40 per cent of all employed women are in clerical occupations and about a further 20 per cent in occupations related to education, health and welfare.[21] In 1975, 46.7 per cent of all female manual workers were employed in catering, cleaning, hairdressing or other personal services. By 1981, this figure had risen to 57.5 per cent.[22] Thus, the much publicised breakthrough of women into non-traditional jobs appears to be more symbolic than significant. If anything, most of the figures above, which are based on census returns, are likely to underestimate the degree of job segregation at establishment level. A 1979 survey of establishments commissioned by the Equal Opportunities Commission found that 66 per cent of men and 36 per cent of women were employed in jobs in which the other sex were not, and had never been, employed.[23] Only 31 per cent of women worked in genuinely integrated jobs, in the sense that not more than 75 per cent of the work force were of one sex.[24]

It is not just that women do different work from men, that their work is horizontally segregated. Within the same broad occupational group, jobs are stratified vertically by sex – that is, men most commonly work in higher grades and women mostly work in lower grades. The 1976 New Earnings Survey, for example, showed that only 4 per cent of women in clerical work can be classified as supervisors, compared with 12 per cent of men. Hakim found that the direction of the trend has been toward greater stratification rather than integration of the sexes. In 1911, women were 24 per cent of skilled workers and 15.5 per cent of unskilled workers. In 1971, only 13.5 per cent of skilled workers were women, whilst the proportion of unskilled workers that were women had risen to 37 per cent. Women, therefore, have become over-represented in the lowest grades of white collar and blue collar work.

Three further findings related to job segregation should be noted. First, research in both Britain and America suggests that the more women in an occupation, the less that occupation pays.[25] There is also clear evidence, in this context, that where the sex composition of jobs has changed from being predominantly male to mainly female, the relative pay has not kept pace. Common examples of this phenomenon include clerical work, bank tellers and telephone operators.

Secondly, in many occupations, part of the difference in average earnings within the occupation can be attributed to the fact that women are more likely than men to be employed in low-paying firms. The Bolton Committee on Small Firms suggested that small enterprises employed more women than large firms and estimated that the difference in earnings between small and large firms was of the order of 20 per cent.[26]

Thirdly, the extent to which occupation accounts for earnings depends on how an occupation is defined. If it is defined broadly, such as in the New Earnings Survey, then differences in pay within the same occupation will be seen as more important than differences between occupations. If an occupation is narrowly defined, in a manner similar to that which would be employed by a 'like work' test under section 1(4) of the Equal Pay Act, then much of the pay differential between men and women can be accounted for by differences in occupation. Failure to make clear this terminological distinction has infused the writings of British labour economists with much confusion.[27]

There is clear evidence, therefore, that part of the earnings gap between men and women results from the concentration of women in low-paying jobs. We turn now to look at the reasons which may explain why jobs are segregated and why there is a link between job segregation and pay differentials.

Classical economics posits that wages are determined directly by the interaction of supply and demand. In reality, however, many workers are employed in medium-sized and large organisations where pay is determined internally through the use of salary structures, job evaluation, and collective bargaining. In such circumstances, the external market may serve as a reference point but no more. Institutional economists have characterised such a system as an 'internal labour market'. Internal labour markets are seen as developing from modern technologies, by which skills have become more firm-specific, so that a worker's productivity increasingly becomes a function of on-the-job training and experience, and consequently of length of service. In such circumstances, it becomes particularly important for the employer to encourage stability and reduce turnover. This is done by providing wages, benefits and prospects better than that which can be obtained in the external market. The internal labour market has a limited number of entry points, mainly at lower job levels, and promotion ladders are commonly attached to jobs. The wage structure tends to reward service with the firm rather than general labour market experience.[28]

Providing more favourable terms and conditions is costly and not all jobs are of the kind where technological change makes stability and on-the-job training important. Accordingly, the labour market can be depicted as segmented into two sectors. The part of the economy characterised by internal labour markets is called the 'primary' sector. The remaining jobs form the 'secondary' sector. The secondary sector includes many jobs requiring little job-specific skill – cleaners, messengers, canteen workers and certain clerical staff may be regarded as examples. In many firms, the two types of jobs may exist side by side. It is suggested that where jobs are such that there is no need for a stable labour force, the external market will be more important and wages will remain low. Since employers in such circumstances will anticipate high turnover, secondary sector jobs are also associated with poor working conditions, lack of skill, little on-the-job training, an absence of promotion opportunities and employment instability. In short, they are 'dead-end' jobs.

That women are over-concentrated in low-paying secondary sector jobs is a matter of fact. Why this occurs, however, is more problematical.

In part, the explanation is that women are excluded from the primary sector in general and, in particular, from higher-paying jobs by discrimination in employment opportunities and job assignment. This is likely to derive from generalisations based on women's higher average turnover.

It is understandable that employers attempt to get the best value out of their investment. In the high-wage primary sector, given the investment made by the firm in training and the cost of defective hiring procedures, employers will attempt to increase the rate of return on their investment by seeking to select employees who are likely to prove stable. Since obtaining accurate information about each individual applicant may be very costly, it is common for employers to utilise a screening device, automatically distinguishing between individuals displaying a particular, readily-ascertainable characteristic which seems to have been associated in the past with employees who meet the particular objective in mind. Sex is a good example of such a screen and if employers believe that women are likely to be less productive or are less likely to be long-term employees than men, they will prefer to hire men for jobs requiring specific training. This is called 'statistical discrimination'.[29]

The effect of 'statistical discrimination' is that individual women who have the desired characteristics (such as stable labour force commitment) are discriminated against inadvertently. They are judged on the basis of group averages. This is unlawful under the Sex Discrimination Act. But, from an economic standpoint, 'statistical discrimination' can be rational behaviour by the employer, both because of the high cost or impracticability of obtaining information about individual workers and because the employer's stereotype about women may be generally accurate (or at least statistically accurate on the basis of the employer's own past experience). Indeed, it is precisely because 'statistical discrimination' is, at least in part, rational behaviour that makes it so difficult for equal opportunities legislation to succeed, for it poses a conflict between the legal aim of each individual being judged on his or her merits and the economic objective of maximising profits.

It is important to note that it is not necessary for the purposes of the 'statistical discrimination' explanation that the employer's beliefs about the characteristics of women be valid in fact, even on an average basis. It is sufficient that the employer believes his preconception to be valid. Audrey Hunt's 1973 survey asked personnel managers whether men were better than women 'at staying with one firm'. The results showed that 43.6 per cent of policy implementers thought men were superior, 15.5 per cent thought women were better.[30] Interestingly, when these figures were up-dated by a survey commissioned by the EOC in 1979, there appeared to be a marked decline in the adverse perception of women. Only 22 per cent now thought that men were better than women 'at staying with one firm' and 19 per cent thought women were superior.[31] Whether this presages a lessening of 'statistical discrimination' remains to be seen. It does suggest, at the least, that employers' stereotypes are being updated in light of women's increased labour force participation.

As a result of employer discrimination, therefore, women with personal characteristics equal to those of men are both channelled into traditionally female jobs and crowded into the low-wage secondary sector. Once there, they become trapped because the process of occupational segregation perpetuates itself. Personnel managers become accustomed to assigning women to traditionally female work and mobility barriers keep the women in such jobs. Women become conditioned to limiting their aspirations to women's work and may develop work habits through feedback which are unsuited to the primary sector. Since women are crowded into women's occupations, there is an over-supply of labour for women's jobs and their wages become depressed relative to that of men with equal productive capacity. Thus the 'market forces' of supply and demand can be regarded as directly attributable to discriminatory job segregation.

Discrimination by employers in recruitment, training and job allocation is not the only explanation for the over-representation of women in the secondary sector. Monopsony theorists point out that because of child-care commitments, married women's job choices will tend to be more constrained than that of their husbands. Thus, married women with children may tend to search for jobs closer to home than do their husbands.[32] This limits their choice, thereby reducing their bargaining power in the market place – that is, they are 'weak sellers' of their labour, unable to hold out for the same pay as the employer must give others for labour that is no better than theirs.[33] The process is reinforced where men join trade unions but women do not.[34] It is also consistent with women being disproportionately employed in small firms. Since there are more small establishments than large, for a married woman whose job choice is constrained by family responsibilities, there is a greater probability of finding a small employer close to home than a large employer.[35]

Although some women are trapped in the secondary sector by lack of choice, there is no doubt that other women more or less voluntarily choose women's jobs in the secondary sector.[36] Doubtless, some women freely choose to prepare for jobs, such as in the 'caring' occupations, where the skills acquired are less marketable than the skills acquired by men, but which may be more satisfying to perform. On the other hand, to what extent younger women follow older women into female-dominated occupations because society has taught them to regard such work as appropriate is unclear.

There is also an economic rationale for women voluntarily choosing secondary sector jobs, notwithstanding their relatively low pay. Training, such as an apprenticeship, can be costly in terms of foregone earnings.[37] Where women expect to marry and have children and do not have an overriding commitment to a work career, their 'prospective discontinuity' may influence them during their pre-maternal employment to acquire less training than men with comparable education and to seek a job that pays the beginner about as much as an experienced worker.[38] If a woman anticipates that she will be out of the labour force for a protracted period in order to bear and raise children, she may choose an occupation in which the job skills gained do not atrophy quickly when not being used. It has been pointed out that those women with the least labour force commitment tend to be in such jobs as primary school teaching, operative, sales and household work where skills depreciate more slowly.[39]

Similarly, when women return to work after having children, family decisions about the division of labour in the household may lead them to choose jobs which offer ease of access, flexibility and convenient hours, and which place less of a premium on continuous service and high attendance – all characteristics of low-paid, secondary sector employment.

Such characteristics are commonly found in part-time work and a particular feature of the 1970s was the enormous growth in part-time employment, especially amongst married women. Between 1971 and 1980, the proportion of women working full-time in Britain remained constant at about 33 per cent. The proportion working part-time rose from 22 per cent to 26 per cent.[40] The overwhelming majority of women working part-time are married.[41] Married women are more likely to work part-time than full-time (56 per cent worked part-time in 1980). The increase in part-time employment amongst women with dependent children has been particularly dramatic. Sixty-eight per cent of women in employment with dependent children worked part-time in 1980 and this accounted for 36 per cent of all women with dependent children (an increase from 26 per cent in 1971, with the proportion of mothers working full-time having risen only from 15 per cent to 17 per cent).[42]

Women working part-time are particularly low paid both in relation to full-time women and to men.[43] The principal reason would seem to be that women who are employed as part-time workers are more likely to be employed on the less skilled jobs.[44]

Taken to its extreme, the jobs women are alleged to choose

voluntarily can be put forward both as an explanation and as a justification for women's lower pay. Thus the CBI, in its evidence to the Royal Commission on the Distribution of Income and Wealth, put forward the following argument:

> A further characteristic of certain lower paid jobs is their higher than average job satisfaction. It would be wrong to assume that all lower paid jobs are unattractive; indeed the nature of some of them can have great appeal. There are for instance many working wives who do not regard their work as a means of maximising household income. In these cases the emphasis placed on the physical proximity of work and perhaps the existence of personal relationships can mean that lower paid jobs possessing those qualities can have a greater attraction than a higher paid one without them. The price of labour in certain lower paid jobs has not been forced up through labour-scarcity because of the existence of a reservoir of people who value aspects associated with these jobs – from mobility and ease of entry and exit, to the very nature of the work itself.[45]

This theory, attributing a high differential amenity value to women's low-paid jobs, is no more than a sophisticated variant of the 'pin money' explanation for why women work. The barely implicit corollary is that if women are not working to maximise income, they don't need to be paid much. Yet the argument doubtless correctly characterises the attitudes of some working women. The point is that there is no reason to believe that it reflects the views of the great majority of women workers. Most women probably choose low-paying jobs because they cannot get high-paying jobs.

We may conclude that there are several different causes for women's disproportionate representation in the low-paid secondary labour market – discrimination by primary sector employers in selection; women's lesser bargaining power in the labour market resulting from constraints on the location of their work and their relatively low degree of unionisation; the voluntary choice of secondary sector jobs, particularly part-time work, because of its greater flexibility. The different causes cannot be disentangled. What is frequently depicted as 'voluntary choice' in reality is circumscribed by the structure of jobs, by the lack of child-care provision and by the division of labour in the family. Discrimination by employers can result in self-confirming behaviour thereby influencing what appears to be self-selection by the women concerned.

What is clear is that differences in occupation between men and women in general, and women's over-representation in secondary sector jobs in particular, account for a substantial part of the earnings gap between the sexes.

Most economists accept that this infers discriminatory recruitment or promotion policies by employers, using the economist's criterion of women holding less well-paid jobs than men for a given level of productivity and experience. But there is a pronounced tendency to classify this as 'employment discrimination' as opposed to 'wage discrimination'. The assumption is that women are paid less than men with equal productive capacity employed in different jobs because the women's jobs are less productive. This is made clear by Chiplin and Sloane when they write: 'Taken to its extreme all wage discrimination is simply job discrimination, since the tasks with different wages can be defined as different jobs.'[46]

There is, however, an alternative possibility: that women in less well-paid jobs are, in fact, equally productive (or, at any rate, that the differences in productivity are not proportionate to the differences in wages), and that what is being observed is not employment discrimination but wage discrimination, in the sense that the value of the women's work is not being correctly rewarded.[47]

The question is one of causation. That women are directed into occupations which are low paying and would not pay any better if they were held by men is one explanation of the pay differences between the sexes. That female-dominated occupations are low paid because they are dominated by women is another hypothesis.

Why should the proportion of women in a job affect its valuation? The short answer is that women's work is undervalued because it is performed by women rather than by men.

THE UNDERVALUATION OF WOMEN'S WORK

The reasons why women's work is undervalued range along a continuum from an obvious prejudice based on stereotyped attitudes about women's role to a much more subtle differentiation of jobs on the basis of status. It is crucial to recognise that prejudice, in the form of a discriminatory animus against women, is not an essential component of discrimination. An employer may undervalue women's work for reasons of expediency – to minimise costs, to avoid industrial relations problems, for example. A similar continuum applies to the ways in which such discrimination is manifested. It may be responsible for blatant changes in the sex composition of jobs to avoid comparisons under the 'like work' provisions of the Equal Pay Act, or it may unconsciously affect the minds of those responsible for implementing job evaluation schemes. The common thread is that the jobs done by women are paid less than they would be if those jobs were done by men.

Although there is little direct evidence,[48] there are substantial reasons for believing that within many organisations women's work is undervalued and that they are discriminated against in terms of pay. Since it was neither unlawful to pay women less for the same work as men or for work of equal value until 1975, this should not be cause for surprise. The Equal Pay Act, which declared the first of these practices unlawful (and provided a remedy for the second where work had been rated as equivalent), changed neither the labour market forces nor the attitudes and prejudices which historically contributed to women's lower pay.

The London School of Economics study of the implementation of the Equal Pay Act in twenty-six organisations[49] provides anecdotal evidence of how employers deliberately attempted to minimise the impact of the 1970 Act by taking steps which had the effect of perpetuating sex-based pay differentials. One strategy which was adopted by employers in response to the Equal Pay Act involved changes to the sex composition of particular jobs or to job duties in order to prevent comparisons under the Act's 'like work' provisions. This could entail moving men (or women) off particular jobs so as to make the job single-sex, thereby precluding a comparison under s.1(4). Whether the resultant segregated jobs are of equal value is an open question dependent on the facts of each case. The other way to achieve the same result was to build into men's jobs sufficient differences in duties to make them no longer 'the same or broadly similar'. Again, although such a strategy has been sufficient to permit an employer to pay unequal wages under s.1(4), the additional duties will only continue to justify unequal pay if they are of greater value than the common core of tasks done. The important point for our purposes here, however, is that to the extent that the sex composition of jobs or job duties were altered in order to avoid paying equal pay for what otherwise would have been equal work, it seems reasonable to suppose that in some cases the work done by the women continued to be of equal value, but was paid less because comparisons were outside the scope of the Act.

More evidence suggesting that women's jobs have been undervalued on grounds of sex derives from grading schemes introduced or modified in order to comply with s.3 of the Equal Pay Act. S.3 provided that collective agreements or pay structures containing any provisions applying specifically to men only or to women only could be referred to the Central Arbitration Committee for amendment to remove that discrimination. Where collective agreements provided for separate and lower women's rates, some firms adopted a strategy of altering the designation of the lowest rate from one relating specifically to women to a unisex grade in practice relating only or predominantly to women's jobs.[50] The recognition that such practices effectively perpetuate the discriminatory undervaluation of women's work was the great contribution made by the CAC, before its powers in this area were effectively circumscribed by the Divisional Court in the *Hy-Mac* case.[51] In its 1977 Annual Report, the Committee pointed out:

> Discrimination does not always appear on the face of the agreement. For example, an agreement may have been renegotiated or altered with Grade 1 and Grade 2 replacing

the previous male clerks and female clerks with no other change. Such a change cannot be said to have ended the matter. The Committee has to ensure that discrimination has been truly removed and replaced with unisex grades bearing appropriate rates.'[52]

Faced with newly unisex grading schemes, the CAC had to distinguish between cases where low rates of pay for women's work accurately reflected job worth and cases where the rate reflected undervaluation because the work was done by women. Analysing the work of the Committee, Paul Davies found that four factors were regarded as evidence for whether discrimination was still present in a pay structure: whether there was a preponderance of men at the top and of women at the bottom of an apparently facially neutral grading structure? Whether there was a history of job segregation by sex? Whether there were very uneven differentials among the rates attached to the various grades in the pay structure? Whether the rate of pay would be likely to attract men?[53] On the basis of these criteria, as Davies reports, nearly all claims that apparently neutral pay structures were discriminatory were upheld by the CAC. Although some of these successful references were in respect of blatant and seemingly deliberate attempts to maintain differentials simply by altering grade designations, the Committee often reached the view that a grading structure was discriminatory despite the employer having taken *bona fide* steps to eliminate discrimination. This, Davies suggests, 'amounts to saying that the discrimination does not flow from prejudice but from status differentiation', that the employer's assessment of what the work is worth to him may be biased by the status of the people who are performing the work.[54]

Economics teaches us that jobs with a high rate of pay will command a high status. Sociology, suggests, however, that the status of the job can determine its pay.[55] Women have lower social status than men so that low status may be ascribed to women's work because it is done by women. Therefore, it has been proposed that women's work is low paid, not merely because of reasons relating to the work or the particular qualifications of those individuals performing it, but, at least in part, simply because the work is performed by women.

Men and women are viewed as having different behavioural characteristics[56] and it is well documented that both men and women place a higher value on the desirability of male, as opposed to female, traits.[57] There is also very strong evidence, deriving from social psychology, that women workers are evaluated as less worthy than male workers with identical characteristics[58] and that male performance is rated more highly than a given female's performance, even when the actual performance is the same.[59] The American National Academy of Science's National Research Council, having surveyed the evidence, reached the conclusion that: 'the evidence for sex stereotyping in job-related contexts is certainly strong enough to suggest the likelihood that sex stereotyping will pervade the evaluation of jobs strongly identified with one sex or the other. That is, it is likely that predominantly female jobs will be undervalued relatively to predominantly male jobs in the same way that women are undervalued relative to men.'[60] Thus the jobs that are performed mainly by women become negatively valued because they are associated with women. They are paid at a lower rate than would be the case if the same jobs were performed predominantly by men.

The contention that there is a link between the fact that most women work in women's jobs and the rates of pay which are associated with those jobs is strengthened by the nature of women's work. Not only is women's work frequently segregated, it is also frequently of a 'feminine' nature. The six occupations where in Britain in 1971 91 per cent or more of the employees were women were typists, secretaries, shorthand writers; maids and related service workers; nurses; canteen assistants, counter hands; hand and machine sewers; and domestic housekeepers.[61] These are occupations which mirror the functions of women inside the home or as male helpmates. Other occupations in which women are prominent require attributes, such as manual dexterity, which the traditional female upbringing fosters.

Since these jobs closely correspond to unpaid housework,

they are not highly valued in an employment context. Negative stereotypes arise so that anything a woman can do is seen as not being worth very much. It is perhaps for this reason that even where men and women do roughly the same kind of work, the posts frequently have different job titles: thus men are 'chefs', women are 'cooks'; men are 'personal assistants', women are 'secretaries'; men are 'salesmen', women are 'shop assistants'. Moreover, an employer who believes that women should be excluded from certain jobs is likely to believe that the segregated jobs women are permitted to perform have less value than the jobs performed by men.[62] The result is that where jobs are identified as being appropriate for women, the very designation carries with it an inference that the jobs are of lesser value than jobs performed by men.[63] It follows that women's jobs are paid less than men's jobs.

It was the policy underlying the Equal Pay Act 1970 that job evaluation should be encouraged as representing a systematic and more objective method of pay determination.[64] Job evaluation, if properly used, by making the criteria for pay explicit and by applying the criteria consistently, can assist in reducing differentials resulting from traditional stereotypes.[65] Yet there is also considerable evidence that job evaluation can simply legitimise the perception of women's work as being of lesser value than that of men. We deal in detail in other sections of this book with discriminatory job evaluation schemes. Suffice it to say here that the inherent subjectivity of job evaluation makes it susceptible to bias, whether intentional or unintentional, at each stage in the process through the inclusion or omission of information relating to particular duties or by undue emphasis on particular duties which favour men at the expense of women. Thus, job analysts lacking familiarity with women's work may underestimate its difficulty.. In writing up the job description, evaluators may disregard skills learned in unpaid work or at home. Skills typically involved in women's work may be ignored in the selection of compensable factors and the values accorded to the relative worth of each factor can emphasise the components of men's jobs.

INEQUALITY OF PAY AND THE LAW

This chapter has shown that there are many causes for the earnings gap between the sexes. It is generally acknowleged that the labour market discriminates against women, but this is just one reason for women's lower pay. Part of the explanation for pay differentials between men and women lies in genuine differences in personal characteristics. Women's qualifications and experience on average are less than men's, largely because women drop out of the labour force to raise children. These differences cannot be entirely wished away by equal pay advocates, although the differences are frequently exaggerated by those purporting to justify inequality, the gap between the sexes is narrowing, the differences in characteristics within each sex are frequently greater than between the sexes and the differences arise in part out of past and present discrimination. In any event, such differences in personal characteristics as exist on average leave most of the pay difference still to be explained and equally qualified women receive substantially less pay than men. It is the differences in jobs that men and women do that seems to offer the fullest explanation for differences in pay. Women are crowded into dead-end jobs in the low-paying secondary sector. Although some women, particularly part-time workers, choose such work because of its greater flexibility, women are also excluded from higher-paying work with better career prospects by discriminatory recruitment and assignment policies. Such policies are based in part on generalisations about women's behaviour which lead employers to discriminate statistically. Added to this, there are reasons for believing that work largely performed by women is paid less than it would be if men were doing the job. The identification of a job with one sex or the other influences its valuation so that women's work is paid less than it ought to be because it is performed by women.

That there are many causes for women's lower pay means that only some of the reasons explaining the earnings gap are susceptible to legal solutions and that there is no single legal solution to which the problem is susceptible. To the extent that women's lower pay is attributable to family responsibilities, the major change required is attitudinal, entailing both the restructuring of work and the division of labour in the family. The law can, at best, smooth the way through provision of child-care facilities and parental leave. To the extent that pay differences result from occupational segregation and the exclusion of women from better-paying jobs, more active use and more effective enforcement of sex discrimination law is what is required, though the value of requiring employers not to discriminate on grounds of sex between equally qualified applicants is limited where women are not as qualified as men. This, in turn, suggests the need for changes in education and career guidance.

Equal pay laws, in and of themselves, can only reduce the earnings gap. They will not eliminate the differential. The 1970 Act dealt with three of the most overt forms of pay discrimination against women: unequal pay for the same job, separate women's rates in collective agreements, and evaluations which were discriminatory on their face. Subsequent to implementation of the Act, the earnings gap was reduced by some 15 per cent, though the extent to which this was because of the legislation remains a subject of controversy.[66]

The new Regulations provide an opportunity to attack the discriminatory undervaluation of women's work. This is another part of the vicious circle of women's economic deprivation. But, even if totally effective, the Regulations offer only a partial solution to this part of the problem. They provide no remedy where segregation is at its worst and there is no male comparator employed on comparable work within the establishment. They provide no recourse for women whose work has been undervalued because of sex but whose work is not of equal value.

Equal pay for work of equal value is a step in the right direction, but too much should not be expected of it. When years after the implementation of equal pay for work of equal value, pay differentials between the sexes remain, it will not necessarily follow that the Regulations have failed.

The extent to which the new Regulations will achieve their limited potential depends principally upon two considerations: how they are utilised and how they are interpreted. Economic principles suggest that firms will comply with employment legislation if the expected costs of violation of the law exceed the costs of compliance with it.[67] Costs, in the context of equal pay for work of equal value, do not simply mean the back pay a Tribunal can award a successful claimant. They include the consequential costs to the employer of disruption to a pay structure by outside intervention, the time costs to management in defending a claim, whether successfully or not (set against the time costs of implementing the Regulations) and any perceived costs in bad publicity and damage to employee moral in being found not to have complied with the law. How the new Regulations are interpreted is obviously crucial and will have a major impact on the extent to which they are utilised. Yet experience under existing discrimination law in both Britain and America strongly suggests that the degree of the law's utilisation affects its interpretation, that the sensitivity and understanding of the judiciary increases according to their exposure to the problem and its dimensions. The more cases that women bring under the new Regulations, the more likely it is that their claims will be successful.

In the remaining sections of this book, we offer guidance on both utilising the new Regulations and on their interpretation.

NOTES

1. *General Household Survey*, 1980, table 6.2. Note, however, that whilst men on average have more formal qualifications, women are more likely than men in most socio-economic groups to have continued their full-time education after leaving school. Ibid, table 6.2.
2. Equal Opportunities Commission, *Annual Report* 1982, table 2.1.
3. Layard *et al.*, *The Causes of Poverty*, Background Paper No. 5, Royal Commission on the Distribution of Income and Wealth, HMSO, 1978, p. 40.
4. M. Corcoran and G. J. Duncan, 'Work history, labor force attachment, and earnings differences beween the races and sexes', *Journal of Human Resources*, vol. 14, Winter 1979, pp. 3–20.
5. The differential varies inversely with educational level.
6. *General Household Survey*, 1980, table 6.6.
7. Michael Evan Gold (*A Dialogue on Comparable Worth*, ILR Press, 1983, p. 6) puts forward the argument with respect to the US that: 'the labor market has been flooded with young women, who have simply

dragged down the average experience and seniority of all working women. Because experience and compensation are correlated, it follows that the average woman today earns less than she did 20 years ago when compared with the average man. Of course, if these women stay in the labor market, their average experience will rise relative to men's, and the women will begin to catch up'.

8. The *General Household Survey*, 1980 (table 5c) shows that 13 per cent of full-time women had changed employers in the twelve months before interview compared with 9 per cent of men.
9. Women do receive less employer-sponsored training than men. A 1979 survey of establishments commissioned by the EOC found that 33 per cent of men were currently taking advantage of training facilities, compared with 25 per cent of women ('Women and Underachievement at Work', *EOC Research Bulletin No. 5*, Spring 1981).
10. 'Family Investments in Human Capital', *Journal of Political Economy*, vol. 82, no. 2, part 2, March–April 1974, pp. 76–108.
11. D. J. Treiman and H. I. Hartmann (eds) *Women, Work, and Wages: Equal Pay for Jobs of Equal Value*, National Academy Press, 1981, p. 18.
12. Ibid, p. 19.
13. H. C. Jain and P. J. Sloane, *Equal Employment Issues: Race and Sex Discrimination in the United States, Canada, and Britain*, Praeger, 1981, p. 56. The authors take the view that this 'could possibly bias the results to indicate . . . sex discrimination'. This is a reasonable point to the extent that women tend to acquire qualifications which are less business-oriented. However set against that is that the non-labour market experience obtained by women as housewives, mothers, etc. is generally entirely discounted by economists.
14. Such as drive, dynamism, determination, enterprise, willingness to take risks and ability to work with others. Henry Phelps Brown, *The Inequality of Pay*, Oxford University Press, 1977, p. 312. For a devastating attack on the accuracy of the techniques used, see George T. Milkovich, 'The Emerging Debate', in E. Robert Livernash (ed.) *Comparable Worth: Issues and Alternatives*, Equal Employment Advisory Council, 1980, pp. 23–47.
15. Jain and Sloane, *Equal Employment Issues*, p. 32.
16. J. F. Madden, 'Economic Rational for Sex Differences in Education', *Southern Economic Review*, April 1978.
17. Michael Webb ('The Labour Market', in I. Reid and E. Wormald (eds) *Sex Differences in Britain*, Grant McIntyre, 1982, p. 164) argues: 'The higher female turnover results in part from the relative youth of the female workforce . . . Most if not all of the remaining differences in turnover can be explained by the fact that women are concentrated into unskilled occupations which have higher turnover rates for both sexes.' Siebert and Sloane ('Shortcomings and Problems in Analyses of Women and Low Pay', in P. J. Sloane (ed.) *Women and Low Pay*, Macmillan, 1980, p. 235) suggest 'it is possible that the higher average

separation rate evinced by women are mainly a consequence of their skill structure. In this case, in fact there might be very little difference between the sexes in their separation rates standardising for skill'. Using American data, Lloyd and Niemi (*The Economics of Sex Differentials*, Columbia University Press, 1979, p. 8) point out: 'Women's records of attendance and labor force turnover are similar to men's when they are compared on the basis of similar job levels and under similar circumstances. Therefore, their higher average rates of turnover relative to men must be explained by the types of jobs they do – jobs which offer less reward in terms of career development and wage growth and which, therefore, provide less incentive to stay for all employees, whether they be men or women.'

Similar arguments have been raised with respect to women's higher average absence rates. Thus Webb ('The Labour Market', p. 163) claims: 'it is well established that low-paid and poorly trained workers, and workers in certain industries, have higher rates of absenteeism, so that differences in rates of absenteeism between the sexes probably reflect the distribution of the sexes by occupation and by industry'. The author of the Department of Employment's *Women & Work: A Review* (DE Manpower Paper No. 11, HMSO, 1975, p. 24) points out: 'It need cause no surprise if the most monotonous low-paid and low-status jobs are those which show the highest absence rates; and if those jobs happen to be filled by women the fact will be reflected in absence rates aggregated by sex.'

18. P. J. Sloane, 'Structure of Labour Markets and Low Pay for Women', in *Women and Low Pay*, p. 138.
19. The relative underpayment of nurses, whose work requires considerable investment in training, is of the highest responsibility and performed in unpleasant working conditions, and has been characterised by repeated staff shortages, is an illustration of the limitations of human capital theory for explaining wage differentials.
20. Catherine Hakim, *Occupational Segregation: A comparative study of the degree and pattern of the differentiation between men's and women's work in Britain, the United States and other countries*, Research Paper No. 9, Department of Employment, 1979, pp. 19–26.
21. B. Chiplin and P. J. Sloane, *Tackling Discrimination at the Workplace: An Analysis of Sex Discrimination in Britain*, Cambridge University Press, 1982, p. 26.
22. EOC, *Annual Report*, 1981.
23. 'Women and underachievement at work', 1981, p. 13. Looking at individual jobs, the survey found that many occupations were largely single-sex. Taking the managerial groups as an example, personnel managers and supervisors of clerks were the only jobs in which a majority of jobs surveyed were desegregated. In comparison, works or production managers were 12 per cent both sexes, 87 per cent men only. Marketing or sales managers were 19 per cent both sexes, 76 per cent men only, 5 per cent women only. In the professional group, the most highly segregated job was that of company secretary (95 per cent

men only, 5 per cent women only). In the intermediate non-manual group, engineering technicians were highly male-dominated (3 per cent both sexes, 97 per cent men only). In the junior non-manual group, there was a marked contrast between clerks, and secretaries and typists. Secretaries and typists were 88 per cent women only, 11 per cent both sexes, 1 per cent men only. Clerks were mainly desegregated (81 per cent both sexes, 1 per cent men only, 18 per cent women only). Lower level jobs in the personal service area were female only. For example, counter hands (13 per cent both sexes, 87 per cent women only). Ibid, p. 18.

24. *Department of Employment Gazette*, November 1980, p. 1144.
25. Sloane (*The Earnings Gap Between Men and Women in Britain*, Social Science Research Council, 1981, p. 10) cites several British research findings that the higher proportion of women in an industry, the lower the wage for both men and women. For the comparable American evidence, see D. J. Treiman and H. I. Hartmann, *Women, Work, and Wages*, p. 28 and *Hearings before The United States Equal Employment Opportunity Commission On Job Segregation And Wage Discrimination*, April 28–30, 1980, p. 398.
26. Cited in B. Chiplin and P. J. Sloane, *Sex Discrimination in the Labour Market*, Macmillan, 1976, p. 46. In the US, Francine Blau (*Equal Pay in the Office*, Lexington Books, 1977) showed that those firms that employed more men in a given occupation than would be expected randomly paid higher than average and those firms that employed more women paid lower than average.
27. See, in particular, the works of Professor Peter Sloane, the most prolific writer on this subject in Britain. Thus, in *The Earnings Gap* (1981, p. 10) and in earlier writings, Sloane asserts that 'wage discrimination' (lower pay for a given job) explains the bulk of the male-female earnings differential. But in Jain and Sloane, *Equal Employment Issues* (1981, p. 235), he asserts that 'pay discrimination' is 'much less important' than employment discrimination in explaining the lower earnings of women.
28. P. B. Doeringer and M. J. Piore, *Internal Labor Markets and Manpower Analysis*, D. C. Heath & Co. 1971. Doeringer, 'Determinants of the Structure of Industrial Type Labor Markets', in *Industrial and Labor Relations Review*, vol. 20, no. 2, January 1967, pp. 206–20. An American study shows that employees in the primary sector are paid 25 to 40 per cent more than other workers (see Gold, *A Dialogue on Comparable Worth*, p. 20).
29. E. S. Phelps, 'The Statistical Theory of Racism and Sexism', *American Economic Review*, vol. 62, no. 4, September 1972, pp. 659–71.
30. A. Hunt, *A Survey of Women's Employment*, Government Social Survey, HMSO, 1968, p. 94.
31. 'Women and Underachievement at Work', *EOC Research Bulletin, No. 5*, Spring 1981.
32. The National Board for Prices and Incomes (Report No. 169, *General Problems of Low Pay*, Cmnd 4648, April 1971) found that the average

journey to work was longer in distance for men than for women. The Equal Opportunties Commission (*Selected Evidence* to the Royal Commission on the Distribution of Income & Wealth, Report No. 6, Lower Incomes, HMSO, 1978, p. 141) has pointed out that unskilled women resuming employment after having a family are more likely to accept employment with low wages because of family need and convenience of location and hours available. 'For these women the responsibility of raising the family was most important.'

33. Phelps Brown, *The Inequality of Pay*, p. 146.
34. P. J. Sloane, *Selected Evidence*, p. 524. In 1980, 38.6 per cent of women in the labour force were trade union members compared with 64.2 per cent of men (EOC, *Annual Report*, 1981). There are reasons for believing that unions may raise women's wages slightly more than those of men when women are covered by a collective agreement. Sloane (*The Earnings Gap*, 1981, p. 25) reports that manual women covered by a collective agreement earned 18.6 per cent more than women not covered (the comparable figure for men being 12.2 per cent). Phelps Brown (*The Inequality of Pay*, pp. 95–6) refers to studies showing that trade unionism has tended to raise the relative pay of the unskilled. Since women are generally in the less skilled category, this also suggests that the absence of coverage by unions is of importance.
35. Chiplin and Sloane, *Tackling discrimination*, 1982, p. 27.
36. To the extent that this is the case, the phrase 'job segregation' is too emotive in that it implies involuntary separation. See Nelson, Opton and Wilson, 'Wage Discrimination and the Comparable Worth Theory in Perspective', *University of Michigan Journal of Law Reform*, vol. 13, no. 2, Winter 1980.
37. J. Mincer and S. Polachek ('Family Investments in Human Capital', *Journal of Political Economy*, vol. 82, 1974) argue that 'a smaller fraction of time and energy is devoted to job advancement (training, learning, getting ahead) per unit of time by persons whose work attachment is lower.'
38. Ibid. See also Gold, *A Dialogue on Comparable Worth*, p. 10.
39. S. Polachek, 'Occupational Segregation: An Alternative Hypothesis', *Journal of Contemporary Business*, Winter 1976. Conversely, women with little time out of the labour force tend to be employed in managerial and professional jobs. However, the empirical evidence is contradictory. Professor Mary Corcoran (*EEOC Hearings*, p. 280), summarising the findings of the US Panel Study of Income Dynamics, has reported: 'The best evidence we were able to get did not seem to support the argument that there was substantial depreciation of women's work skills during periods of non-work.'
40. *General Household Survey*, 1980, tables 5.2 and 5.3.
41. *EOC Research Bulletin*, vol. 1, no. 1, Winter 1978–9.
42. *General Household Survey*, 1980.
43. Sloane and Siebert ('Low Pay amongst Women – the Facts', *Women and Low Pay*, 1980, p. 24), studying a range of occupational groups, found that in every occupation but one and in every industry where

data were available, a higher percentage of part-timers than full-timers were low paid.

44. Hunt's survey in 1965 (*Survey of Women's Employment*, pp. 32–3 and table A19) found that full-time women workers at that time outnumbered part-timers by nearly two to one. But amongst personal service workers, 59.5 per cent were part-timers and only 36.5 per cent of women were full-timers. Amongst unskilled manual workers, some 78 per cent of women were employed part-time. In contrast, 85 per cent of professional and managerial occupations were filled by full-timers. Hunt also found that a majority of women working part-time did so because of various kinds of domestic responsibilities and most said that they would not work longer hours under any circumstances. Ibid, pp. 36–8.
45. Sloane, *Selected Evidence*, p. 109.
46. Chiplin and Sloane, *Tackling discrimination*, p. 58.
47. Wage discrimination would amount to 'exploitation' – payment to the worker of less than his or her marginal revenue product – and such a concept, although acknowledged, does not fit easily into the neoclassical model.
48. Economists using the adjustment method of explaining pay differences have regarded the extent of the differential left unexplained after accounting for other variables, including occupation and personal characteristics, as attributable to discrimination. Such an approach may be suggestive of discrimination but it is fraught with difficulties. As we noted above, it is impossible to take account of differences in personal characteristics accurately, it is difficult to define differences in occupation clearly and there are few studies, in any event, at the level of the firm. See Milkovich, 'The Emerging Debate'.
49. M. W. Snell, P. Glucklich and M. Povall, *Equal Pay and Opportunities*, Department of Employment Research Paper No. 20, April 1981.
50. At the time of the Act's implementation, this was viewed in some circles as being an acceptable way of complying with the Act's requirements. Thus the Office of Manpower Economics, in its 1972 report *Equal Pay* (para. 49), classified as 'removing discrimination', the 'elimination of separate rates for women either by raising existing rates to the corresponding rates for men or by replacing women's rates by new occupational designations'.
51. *R.* v. *Central Arbitration Committee ex parte Hy-Mac Ltd* [1979] IRLR 461.
52. Para. 2.16.
53. P. L. Davies, 'The Central Arbitration Committee and Equal Pay', *Current Legal Problems 1980*, p. 175.
54. Ibid, p. 175 and Note 33, p. 190.
55. Barbara Wootton (*The Social Foundations of Wage Policy*, 1955) points out: 'what is anomalous to the economist may make perfectly good sense to the sociologist. In a hierarchical society such as ours, large issues of social status are involved in wage and salary scales. Pay and prestige are closely linked; and (in spite of some exceptions) it is

the rule that the high prestige person should be also the highly-paid person; and vice versa'. See also Phelps Brown, *The Inequality of Pay*, p. 179.

56. *EEOC Hearings*, 1980, p. 147, testimony of Professor Ann Viviano. Men are seen as more achieving, active, striving, intelligent, powerful and independent; women are seen as gentle, sensitive, passive and dependent – qualities which are not normally regarded as suitable for jobs of importance.
57. J. S. King, *Women and Work: Sex Differences and Society*, DE Manpower Paper No. 10, HMSO, 1974, p. 20, reports a 1957 study by McKee and Sheriffs which asked 85 men and 93 women to list 10 characteristics of men and 10 characteristics of women on a 200-adjective checklist. These 200 adjectives had previously been rated for desirability by a group evenly split between men and women. An examination of those adjectives chosen as 'masculine' and 'feminine' demonstrated that both sexes considered that men possessed the more favourable characteristics and women the less favourable characteristics.
58. Treiman and Hartmann (eds) *Women, Work, and Wages*, p. 77. *EEOC Hearings*, Ann Viviano, 1980, p. 151.
59. King, *Women and Work*, p. 20. A. Viviano, *EEOC Hearings*, p. 151.
60. Treiman and Hartmann (eds) *Women, Work, and Wages*, p. 78.
61. Hakim, *Occupational Segregation*, p. 31. Amongst the other 'feminine' occupations in which women are greatly over-represented are charwomen, office cleaners; hairdressers, manicurists; kitchen hands; launderers, dry cleaners; and housekeepers, matrons.
62. W. Newman and J. Vonhof, '"Separate But Equal" – Job Segregation and Pay Equity In The Wake of *Gunther*', *University of Illinois Law Review*, vol. 1981, no. 2, p. 271.
63. Ruth Blumrosen, 'Wage Discrimination, Job Segregation, and Title VII of the Civil Rights Act of 1964', *University of Michigan Journal of Law Reform*, vol. 12, 1979, p. 247. This is the seminal article on the 'comparable worth' theory in America.
64. See Barbara Castle, *Hansard*, House of Commons, 22.4.70.
65. Treiman and Hartmann (eds) *Women, Work, and Wages*, p. 95.
66. It has been suggested that the reduction in differentials was mainly due to the effects of Government incomes policy in the period 1972–5. Incomes policy provided for flat-rate pay increases, which had the effect of compressing skill differentials, thereby raising the relative earnings of women who are concentrated in low-paid unskilled job classifications (see Sloane, *Selected Evidence*, p. 521). Thus, Chiplin, Curran and Parsely ('Relative Female Earnings in Great Britain and Legislation', in P. J. Sloane, *Women and Low Pay*, p. 115) found that on the assumption that incomes policy limits were not exceeded, two of the eight percentage points in the narrowing of the differential in this period could be explained by equal pay legislation or other factors, with six percentage points due to Government incomes policy. On the

other hand, Layard *et al*. ('The Causes of Poverty', 1978, p. 53) attribute the change to the Equal Pay Act:

> It is sometimes said that the change is due mainly to the flat rate nature of incomes policy wage increases . . . This argument is wrong. It would only be true if the increases in question would not have come about without the incomes policy. For this to be true it is necessary that the incomes policies were binding, i.e., they forced employers to pay women more than they otherwise would and presumably men less than they otherwise would. But in fact the evolution of pay in recent years had been only marginally related to incomes policy . . . In general women as well as men have got more than the policy stipulated and in fact the statutory policies of 1973–4 allowed progress to equal pay outside the pay limits. Moreover, in 1974/5 there was a period of free collective bargaining which could quite well have undone the effects of previous incomes policies even if these had been binding. It is noticeable that women made sharp gains relative to men between April 1974 and April 1975, during half of which period there was free collective bargaining.

The entire issue, in any event, is clouded by the inability to hold constant other factors at work during the period. Thus, in the US, the earnings differential between the sexes has not decreased at all since the enactment of equal pay legislation in 1963. This has sometimes been regarded by British commentators as indicating that the US law was defective, but American researchers have pointed out that during this period there has been a marked increase in women's labour force participation. Andrea Beller ('Title VII and the Male/Female Earnings Gap: An Economic Analysis', *Harvard Women's Law Journal*, vol. 1, no. 1, Spring 1978, pp. 157–73) argues that 'new entrants into the labor market have typically had less work experience than those who are already in the labor market and, therefore, they command lower wages. Taken alone, the rapid increase in the labor force participation of women tends to increase the earnings differential. The fact that the earnings differential remained constant in face of this significant trend suggests that something else is working to decrease the differential', and that the male/female earnings gap would have increased had it not been for the enforcement of the legislation (see also Lloyd and Niemi, *The Economics of Sex Differentials*, pp. 10–11). A similar analysis can be applied to the British experience.

67. Beller, 'Title VII and the Male/Female Earnings Gap'.

3 The Legislative Context

The Equal Pay Act 1970 provides a right to equal pay for 'like work', defined by s.1(4) as work which is 'the same' or of a 'broadly similar nature', and a right to equal pay for 'work rated as equivalent', defined by s.1(5) as where the jobs compared 'have been given an equal value, in terms of the demand made on a worker under various headings (for instance effort, skill, decision) on a study undertaken with a view to evaluating in those terms the jobs to be done by all or any of the employees in an undertaking or group of undertakings'.

The 1970 Act represented a conscious compromise by the Labour Government between a standard of equality limited to 'equal pay for equal work' as embodied in Article 119 of the Treaty of Rome and the broader standard of 'equal pay for work of equal value' as suggested by ILO Convention 100.[1] The EEC standard of equal pay for equal work was thought by the Government to be 'too narrow, too restrictive'. Therefore, by adding the extension 'broadly similar', the Treaty of Rome definition was widened 'beyond the concept of a woman being engaged on like work with a man'.[2]

The Government's stated reasons for rejecting equal pay for work of equal value were that the concept was too abstract and that it would require a nationwide job evaluation. Introducing the Bill, Mrs Barbara Castle pointed out:

> The phrase 'Equal pay for work of equal value' is too abstract a concept to embody in legislation without further interpretation. Is it suggested that some one should set a value on every job a woman does? Even if that were practicable it would not solve the problem, because what we are concerned with is the relationship between men's pay and women's pay, and men, of course, have never had

> equal pay for work of equal value. One could only establish the relative value of men's and women's work by evaluating the work, not only of all women but of all men in the population, which is something we have never attempted in our wildest dreams of prices and incomes policies.[3]

Underlying this objection was the view that job evaluation posed the danger of upsetting wage differentials between men.[4] Baroness Phillips, the Government spokesman in the House of Lords, warned that:

> In order to assess the value of women's work it would be necessary to evaluate the jobs not only of all women, but also of men in the working population, as only in this way could the relative value of men's and women's work be satisfactorily established. Such an operation would be quite impracticable, if only because there are insufficient trained staff available to do the evaluation. But even if it were possible, it would not be desirable because it could have the incidental effect of upsetting pay differentials between men, and it is no part of the Government's purpose to do this.[5]

When the UK joined the EEC in 1972, European Community law became part of the law of Britain.[6] In October 1972, the European Commission was asked by the heads of state to draw up a Social Action Programme. Amongst the priority proposals of that plan, announced in October 1973, was a Directive, binding on Member States, 'providing for the approximation of legislation of Member States concerning the application of the principle of equal pay for men and women'.[7]

The Commission originally proposed that the Directive define equal pay in terms of equal pay for work of equal value, but due to objections from the UK Government, the definition was altered.[8] Article 1 of the Equal Pay Directive (75/117 of 10 February 1975) defined the principle of equal pay as meaning 'for the same work or for work to which equal value is attributed, the elimination of all discrimination on grounds of sex with regard to all aspects and conditions of remuneration'. Article 1 goes on to state that: 'In particular, where a job classification system is used for determining pay, it must be based on the same criteria for both men and women and so drawn up as to exclude any discrimination on grounds of sex.' Article 2 of the Directive requires Member States to 'introduce into their national legal systems such measures as are necessary to enable all employees who consider themselves aggrieved by the non-application of the principle of equal pay to pursue their claims by judicial process after possible recourse to other competent authorities.'

The UK, although accepting the Directive, nonetheless, at the final Council of Ministers' meeting when the Directive was approved, insisted on placing on record its view that 'the circumstances in which work is concerned to have had equal value attributed to it' within the meaning of Article 1, 'are where the work is broadly similar, or where pay is based on the results of job evaluation'.[9] This accorded with the UK Government's understanding of the provisions of the British Equal Pay Act and was clearly designed to avoid the prospect of the UK being held to be out of compliance with the Directive.

That prospect became a reality in 1979 when the European Commission, having studied the implementation of the Directive,[10] announced that it was to take infringement proceedings against seven Member States, including the UK, for not fully complying with the Directive. The principal complaint against the UK concerned what the Commission termed 'the restrictive interpretation' given to the concept of 'work of equal value' by s.1(5) of the Equal Pay Act.[11] The effect of this, the Commission argued, was that a woman employed on work of equal value to that of a man could not obtain equal pay unless a job evaluation scheme was applied by the employer.

The application was heard by the European Court of Justice on 23 March 1982. As well as pointing to its statement made at the time the Directive was adopted, the UK Government argued that the Directive refers only to the need for equal pay where equal value 'is attributed' to the work, rather than simply where work is 'of equal value'. Therefore, the UK contended, the Directive did not provide a right for employees to insist upon some form of job evaluation being carried out. The UK also took the view that to implement a system of equal pay for work of equal value would entail practical problems and that the concept was too abstract to be applied by the courts.[12]

These arguments were rejected by the European Court of Justice, which, on 6 July 1982, allowed the application and declared that: 'by failing to introduce into its national legal system in implementation of the provisions of Council Directive No 75/117/EEC of 10.2.75 such measures as are necessary to enable all employees who consider themselves wronged by failure to apply the principle of equal pay for men and women for work to which equal value is attributed and for which no system of job classification exists to obtain recognition of such equivalence, the United Kingdom has failed to fulfil its obligations under the Treaty'. The Court reasoned that implementation of the Directive's principle of equal pay for work of equal value required that a worker must be entitled to claim equal pay before an appropriate judicial authority regardless of the employer's wishes, and any method which excluded that option prevented the aims of the Directive from being achieved.

In August 1982, the Government sent to interested parties a specification for amending the Equal Pay Act to give effect to the European Court's decision,[13] and in November the Government announced that the Act would be amended by means of an Order under s.2 of the European Communities Act 1972. S(2) of that Act allows a designated Minister to implement a European Community obligation by Order and s.2(4) enables such an Order to amend an Act of Parliament. In order to understand why the Government chose this approach, rather than that of implementing the Court's decision by means of amending legislation, it must be borne in mind that the Government resisted the infringement proceedings and clearly wished to do no more than was necessary to comply with EEC law. The difference between the Equal Pay Act and the EEC Directive was characterised by the Under Secretary of State for Employment (Mr Alan Clark) as 'a small gap' which needed to be closed and he claimed that 'the European Communities Act 1972 provides a means to do this swiftly and efficiently by regulations'.[14] This procedural decision, however, had three important ramifications. A draft Order can only be accepted in full or rejected in full by Parliament; it cannot be amended. Secondly, an Order made under the European Communities Act can only give effect to a European obligation; it cannot make any other substantive changes to the law. Thirdly, the procedure adopted ensured that Parliamentary debate on the Regulations would be limited to a single opportunity of about 90 minutes' debate in each House to approve or reject the Order.

A consultative Draft Order was published in February 1983. It was severely criticised by the Equal Opportunities Commission and by women's groups and it was argued that the proposals would not meet the requirements of European law.[15]

In July 1983, the Government laid a final Draft Order before Parliament, to come into force on 1 January 1984.[16] The Order met some of the criticisms which had been made of the original proposals. The defence under s.1(3) where there had been a finding of work of equal value in its original form would have required the applicant to show that the variation in pay was sexually discriminatory. This was altered so that the burden of proving the defence remained on the employer throughout, but the Order distinguished between the defence to a like work or work rated as equivalent claim – where the employer must show that the variation is due to a material factor which must be a material difference 'between the woman's case and the man's' – and an equal value claim, where the material factor does not have to be a material difference between the woman's case and the man's. In addition, the original proposal to preclude claims where work had already been evaluated as being unequal was changed so as to permit claims in such circumstances if the employer's evaluation was sexually discriminatory. The Regulations were approved by the House of Commons on 20 July after a brief but stormy debate, in which the language of the Regulations was criticised as being 'incomprehensible'.[17]

In order to implement the new Regulations, it was necessary to amend the Industrial Tribunal Rules of Procedure and in particular to set out the role of the independent expert. The amending Regulations provide that an Industrial Tribunal cannot determine an equal value claim until it has received an independent expert's report, and during the Commons' debate the Minister had stated that the Procedural Regulations would provide that once the expert had reported, the parties would be limited to making representations on the report and would not be permitted to cross-examine the expert. When the Government issued its draft proposals to this effect in September 1983, once more there was heavy criticism[18] and it was contended that the draft Rules would not be in accordance with the obligations imposed by EEC law to ensure that the right to equal pay is determined by a fair and effective judicial process to which the claimant has unhindered access.

Now the Government was getting caught up in the procedural web it had spun for itself. The complexity of the amending Regulations were producing a stream of articles and correspondence in legal journals suggesting that the language used was technically defective.[19] They could not be amended and had already been passed by the House of Commons. Doubt had also been cast on the draft Procedural Regulations which, in turn, had been based on the amending Regulations. The debate in the House of Lords on the amending Regulations, scheduled for the end of October, was postponed at the last moment amidst rumours that the Regulations would be withdrawn. In the event, it was not until 5 December that the debate was held, by which time the Government had revised the Procedural Regulations to permit parties to cross-examine the independent expert and to call an alternative expert witness. Lord Gowrie assured the House of Lords that 'it will be apparent that the expert can be challenged and that his report is simply evidence on the question of the value of the jobs at issue. It is for the Tribunal to decide what weight to attach to all the evidence, and ultimately to decide the issue'.[20] None the less, the House of Lords took the unusual step of attaching an amendment to the motion to approve the Regulations which stated 'that this House believes that the Regulations do not adequately reflect the 1982 decision of the European Court of Justice and Article 1 of the EEC Equal Pay Directive of 1975'.[21]

The Procedural Regulations were laid before Parliament on 9 December,[22] subject to negative resolution. Meanwhile, Lord Gowrie's statement was referred to the Parliamentary Joint Committee on Statutory Instruments to determine whether it was 'compatible' with the language of the Procedural Regulations. On 17 January 1984, the Committee issued its report declaring that the special attention of Parliament did not need to be drawn to the situation. But the Committee concluded that 'the status afforded to the expert's report is not made clear by the Procedural Regulations, which should have provided further elucidation'.[23] By this time, the Order bringing the Procedural Regulations into force had been prayed against in both Houses. This resulted in debates on 1 February 1984 during which both the language and substance of the Regulations were again attacked. The tortuous legislative saga came to an end when the motion to annul the Regulations was withdrawn in the House of Lords and defeated in the House of Commons.

NOTES

1. Article 2(1) of that Convention states: 'Each Member shall . . . ensure the application to all workers of the principle of equal remuneration for men and women workers for work of equal value.'
2. Equal Pay (No. 2) Bill, Standing Committee H, 24.2.70, Col 64 (Mrs Barbara Castle). According to Mrs Castle: 'The CBI was all in favour of the definition embodied in the Treaty of Rome . . . but the TUC emphatically rejected this as inadequate. The TUC wanted the IL Convention . . . which the CBI, in turn, rejected as being far too open ended and indefinite. I think they both were right. "Equal pay for the same work" is so restrictive that it would merely impinge on those women, very much in the minority, who work side by side with men on identical work, while the IL definition is far from satisfactory.' *Hansard*, House of Commons, 9.2.70, col. 915.
3. Ibid, col. 916.
4. C. A. Larsen, 'Equal pay for women in the United Kingdom', *International Labour Review*, vol. 103, no. 1, January 1971, p. 3.
5. *Hansard*, House of Lords, 5.5.70, col. 122.

6. S.2 of the European Communities Act 1972 provides that European Community law shall 'be enforced, allowed and followed' in the UK and that 'any enactment passed or to be passed . . . shall be construed and have effect subject to' that principle.
7. *European Industrial Relations Review*, Preview Edition, December 1973, pp. 2 and 24.
8. EIRR 12, December 1974.
9. EIRR 13, January 1975.
10. The full text of the Commission's draft report appears in EIRR 58, November 1978.
11. EIRR 64, May 1979. For a good discussion of the background to the infringement proceedings, see Rights of Women Europe, *Women's Rights & the EEC: A Guide for Women in the UK*, 1983.
12. [1982] IRLR 333.
13. Department of Employment, *Specification for amending the Equal Pay Act to provide for equal pay for men and women for work to which equal value is attributed.* This initial discussion document placed considerable emphasis on the parties agreeing voluntarily to a job evaluation study with the assistance of ACAS to establish the relative value of the jobs concerned. Only if such a voluntary evaluation could not be carried out successfully would the Tribunal appoint an 'independent assessor'.
14. *Hansard*, House of Commons, 20.7.83, col. 480.
15. See Equal Opportunities Commission, *Leading Counsel's Opinion on the proposed amendments to the Equal Pay Act 1970.*
16. S.I. 1983 No. 1794.
17. *Hansard*, House of Commons, 20.7.83.
18. For a wide-ranging and cogent critique, see Anthony Lester, 'Unequal Pay – Unequal Justice', *New Law Journal*, 28 October, 1983.
19. See the editorials and correspondence in the *New Law Journal* during August, September and October 1983, including the present author's letter of 26 August. See also, Michael Rubenstein, 'Discriminatory Job Evaluation Schemes and the Equal Pay (Amendment) Regulations', *New Law Journal*, 18 November, 1983.
20. *Hansard*, House of Lords, 5.12.83, col. 926.
21. Ibid, col. 886.
22. S.I. 1983 No. 1807.
23. *Thirteenth Report from the Joint Committee on Statutory Instruments*, Session 1983–4.

4 The Scope of Claims

This chapter looks at the scope of equal pay for work of equal value claims. The Equal Pay Act itself places significant limitations on the kinds of claims which can be brought under the new Regulations. But, as we shall see, the scope for claims is much wider than might be apparent at first thought.

COMPARISON MUST BE WITH THE OPPOSITE SEX

A claim for equal pay for work of equal value must be based on a comparison with a person of the opposite sex. The Equal Pay Act is a statute aimed at remedying discrimination in pay based on sex; it does not purport to mandate fairness in pay generally. The amended Act, therefore, continues to require that a woman can only claim equal pay with a man and a man can only claim equal pay with a woman.[1] A woman cannot compare herself with another woman and a man cannot compare himself with another man. Of course, if a claim is successful, there may well be repercussions for the pay of both sexes (in that men employed on equal work with a successful woman complainant consequently will be able to claim the woman's new rate, and other women in that grade employed on equal work with those men thereupon will have a consequential claim for their pay to be increased). But an Industrial Tribunal will only adjudicate on a claim for equal pay for work of equal value with a person of the opposite sex.

SAME EMPLOYMENT

A second limitation is that the 'comparator' – the person of the opposite sex paid higher with whom the comparison is made – must be employed in 'the same employment' as the claimant.

S.1(6) of the Act provides that 'men shall be treated as in the same employment with a woman if they are men employed by her employer or any associated employer at the same establishment or establishments in Great Britain which include that one and at which common terms and conditions of employment are observed either generally or for employees of the relevant classes'. The thrust of this limitation is that, at its broadest, a claim can be made between a woman and a man in different parts of a corporate group. A comparison *cannot* be made with men in other firms in the industry or in the same geographical area.

This much is clear. However, the next stage, ascertaining the precise meaning of the definition in s.1(6) so as to discover how far within the corporate group claims can be brought, is an exceptionally complex exercise.

The first question is whether the claimant and her comparator are employed in the same 'establishment'. There is no definition of 'establishment' either in the Equal Pay Act or in any other employment legislation, so how are we to determine whether a chain of shops or a group of building sites or offices in different geographical locations constitute one establishment? Although there is no statutory definition, the term 'establishment' is used in the redundancy consultation provisions of the Employment Protection Act 1975, s.99(3) of which makes the minimum consultation provisions contingent upon the proposed redundancies being at 'one establishment'. The only appellate court consideration of the term came in *Barratt Developments (Bradford) Ltd v. UCATT*,[2] where the EAT, in upholding the Industrial Tribunal's decision that fourteen housebuilding sites administered from one base amounted to one establishment rather than fourteen separate establishments, took the view that: 'upon the normal canons of construction that word is intended to convey what it means to ordinary people . . . it is what "establishment" means to the Industrial Tribunal, functioning, as it has been aptly said to function, as an industrial jury, that in truth Parliament intended it to mean'. 'Establishment' was also a term used in the legislation on Selective Employment Tax. Although in *Barratt Developments* the EAT expressly rejected the use of case law under the Selective Employment Tax as setting *precedents* for the meaning of the term in other employment legislation, the *criteria* used in SET cases do provide guidance.[3] They were so used by the Industrial Tribunal in the redundancy consultation case of *Bakers' Union v. Clarks of Hove Ltd*,[4] in finding that employees working in a bakery, a factory and twenty-eight retail shops were all employed at one establishment. The Industrial Tribunal noted that the SET cases 'indicated that no one exclusive or comprehensive test was available, but that a number of factors might be relevant in determining the scope of an "establishment", e.g. location in relation to other premises of the employer, separate management, separate accounting, separation of services and separation of profits'.

In short, an 'establishment' is by no means synonymous with a physically separate place of business. On the contrary, organisation of management appears to be the most important determinant, so that if a group of different geographical sites are all managed and controlled from one location, it is likely that they will be held to form one establishment so permitting equality claims between women and men employed at different locations within the establishment – for example, between managers of separate retail outlets controlled by a regional headquarters.

If there is not one establishment, a woman can still claim that she is employed on work of equal value with a man in a different establishment of the company, provided that 'common terms and conditions of employment are observed either generally or for employees of the relevant classes' between the two establishments. Once again, whether there are common terms and conditions is largely a question of fact and degree, but two points should be borne in mind: first, that there is a difference in pay rates (or any other term or condition) between two establishments does not necessarily negate there being common terms and conditions since that would render the section meaningless. Secondly, it is sufficient that there be common terms and conditions between the two establishments for the classes of employees who are the subject of the claim – e.g. managerial grades. To take a broad rule of thumb, if pay and conditions for different establishments are negotiated or determined centrally, we would expect to find common terms and conditions at least within the same bargaining unit. If different establishments determine pay and conditions autonomously and there are important variations between them, it is unlikely that there will be 'common terms and conditions'.

Finally, whether common terms and conditions exist between establishments determines whether a claim can be brought rather than corporate structure. S.1(6) extends the scope for equality claims to 'associated employers', provided common terms and conditions exist. Two employers are defined as associated 'if one is a company of which the other (directly or indirectly) has control or if both are companies of which a third person (directly or indirectly) has control'.

That the comparator must be of the opposite sex and must be employed in the same employment are two limitations on the claims that can be brought. Of equal interest, however, is the absence of limitations on claims in several significant respects.

CLAIMS ACROSS EXISTING PAY BOUNDARIES

First, claims can be brought across the existing boundaries of bargaining units, grading systems or job evaluation schemes. The existence of separate pay systems for manual workers and clerical staff, for example, will not stop a woman clerical worker claiming that she is employed on work of equal value with a male manual worker. Similarly, that union *A* has negotiated a packet of terms and conditions for one group cannot preclude workers in a second group, where a different set of terms and conditions were negotiated by union *B*, from bringing a claim for equality. To allow such comparisons to be made is central to the underlying philosophy of the Regulations and if there is a finding of work of equal value, differences in negotiating groups or in grading systems or in evaluation schemes may not, in and of themselves, be acceptable defences.

HIGH VULNERABILITY AREAS

There are several circumstances in which employers may be most vulnerable to equal value claims. The first is the 'almost' like work case, comparisons which are 'near misses' under the like work provisions of the Equal Pay Act. This would cover circumstances where the man and the woman are doing similar work, but there are sufficient differences in the tasks performed to take the two jobs outside the scope of s.1(4). In some cases, these differences may have originated in a deliberate attempt to mitigate the effects of the 1970 Act, such as where the man was given extra duties in addition to the common core of tasks which he and the woman perform.

There are two significant distinctions in this context between the like work test and the test for work of equal value. Under the like work test, where two jobs have a common core of tasks but the man also performs additional duties, those differences in duties in and of themselves may have been sufficient to defeat a claim. Under the equal value test, a claim will only be defeated if the man's additional duties require greater skill, effort or responsibility. Differences in duties will justify unequal pay only if the additional duties the man performs are not simply different, but are of greater value than the common core of duties which both sexes perform. Secondly, under the like work test, effectively the two jobs being compared must be of equal skill, require equal effort and demand equal responsibility. The greater responsibility of, say, the woman's job cannot be offset against the greater effort of the man's job. Under equal pay for work of equal value, this balancing should take place because it is the overall skill, effort and responsibility required by the two jobs that is being weighed.

This leads to the second kind of case which can be brought under the new Regulations: what can be termed 'comparable worth'. This is the case where there are not substantial similarities in the tasks performed, but nevertheless the two jobs may be of equal value. This is really the principal focus of the Regulations; the kind of claim that now must be adjudicated in order to comply with the European Court's ruling. The Regulations, for the first time, allow a woman who works in a 'women-only' job to bring a claim that she is being discriminated against in terms of pay, at least to the extent that she is not paid equally with a man employed on work of equal value. Previously, women in women-only jobs had no remedy because there was no man doing the same work to serve as a comparator. Now, these women can point to men doing different work, but work which is of equal value.

A different area where employers may be particularly vulnerable is in respect of workers outside existing evaluation schemes. Employees who are outside the scope of an evaluation scheme because their evaluated worth would require the employer to pay more than the market dictates should be amongst the prime beneficiaries of the equal value Regulations. Canteen staff, who are frequently outside the scope of collective agreements and paid less than labourers for what may be comparable work, may fall within this category. Industrial nurses may be another example. Similarly, where secretarial staff have been graded or evaluated separately, comparisons may be made with other white collar staff.

This brings us to the problem which is the converse of that just discussed: where a group of workers is outside the evaluation scheme because their evaluated worth would be less than the rate of pay required in order to attract them in sufficient numbers. Computer programmers are the classic example. One of the central issues under the Regulations will be the extent to which employers will continue to be able to pay unequal pay for work of equal value because of the dictates of the labour market. We look at this issue in Chapter 8.

ANY TERM OR CONDITION

The Equal Pay Act relates to any and all contractual terms and conditions of employment (with the single exception of provisions relating to death or retirement – i.e. pension benefits, which are specifically excluded).[5] An equal value claim, therefore, does not have to be a claim for equal basic wage rates. It can be a claim for equality with respect to another aspect of remuneration, such as a bonus scheme. It can also be a claim based on unequal treatment with regard to a non-wage contractual term or condition, such as sick pay benefits or subsidised mortgage schemes.

The amended s.1(2)(c) of the Act provides that where a woman is employed on work of equal value to that of a man, then

> (i) if (apart from the equality clause) any term of the woman's contract is or becomes less favourable to the woman than a term of a similar kind in the contract under which that man is employed, that term of the woman's contract shall be treated as so modified as not to be less favourable, and
>
> (ii) if (apart from the equality clause) at any time the woman's contract does not include a term corresponding to a term benefiting that man included in the contract under which he is employed, the woman's contract shall be treated as including such a term.

These words are directly parallel to those in the existing s.1(2) of the Act where there is a finding of like work or work rated as equivalent. But where a man and a woman are employed on broadly similar work or on work rated as equivalent under an established job evaluation scheme, it is highly probable that they will enjoy pretty much the same conditions and benefits. In contrast, the comparisons that may be made under the equal value provisions may be between completely different grades of workers or different negotiating groups. Indeed, it may be the difference in other aspects of remuneration or in non-wage contractual fringe benefits that underlies the claim. Consider the effect of the equality clause in such circumstances. The equality clause does not simply require that the terms overall be no less beneficial as between the man and the woman. It requires that each and every term or condition be the same. 'Any' less favourable term of the woman's contract must be modified as to be not less favourable. Unless the employer can establish a defence to the claim under the amended s.1(3), therefore, once there is a finding that a woman and a man are employed on work of equal value, they will have to be given not only the same basic rate, but also the identical package of overall contractual terms and conditions.

In the event, much will depend on whether the employer can establish that the variation in conditions is based on a factor other than the difference of sex. Where there are status distinctions drawn on an overall basis between manual workers and staff, a defence that the difference is not sex-based should prove to be acceptable. But what of the case where an aspect of remuneration is, in reality, a device to ensure that men's work is paid more than women's work? Are there differences in the work done which can justify including men's jobs within an incentive bonus scheme and not covering women's jobs, despite the work being of equal value? What of the cases where differences in fringe benefits are, in reality, tainted by sex? On what basis can an employer justify the failure to include canteen staff within a sick pay scheme or a subsidised mortgage scheme for which secretaries are not eligible?

There is a further complication of great potential importance deriving from the wording of s.1(2)(c). Once an equality clause operates, any term of the woman's contract is modified by law so as to be not less favourable than that of her male comparator. Take the case of a woman chargehand claiming equal pay with a male clerical supervisor. Her work is found to be of equal value. The employer now argues his defence. We would anticipate that what he is going to attempt to justify is the difference in pay, since that is the basis of the claim. If that is all he does and he is unsuccessful, what will the result be? Not only will the woman's pay be increased, but all other aspects of her terms and conditions will be automatically modified in consequence. These may include variations in contractual fringe benefits which the employer did not attempt to justify because they were not the focus of the complaint. Some of these differences, say a difference in sick pay arrangements, may have been justifiable as not being sex-based, even if the difference in pay was not. S.1(3) permits the employer to defend 'a' variation between the woman's contract and the man's contract. This means *any* variation, so that it would appear that an employer can argue that even if pay is equalised, sick pay benefits should not be because *that* variation is due to a material factor other than sex. Unless employers are prepared to defend separately each and every variation in terms and conditions, those terms and conditions will automatically be altered as a consequence of an equal pay claim succeeding.

In practical terms, therefore, the wording of the equality clause in s.1(2)(c) could prove to be one of the most explosive aspects of the new law. It may generate substantial numbers of claims and pose severe problems of implementation for management.

MULTIPLE COMPARISONS

Both the amended Act and the amended Industrial Tribunals (Rules of Procedure) Regulations refer in the singular to a comparison between an individual woman and an individual man. In practice, however, this may not be the way in which some claims are framed.

The discriminatory undervaluation of women's work may be regarded as primarily a class issue, in that it is women's work generally, or at least the work of a group of women, which is undervalued rather than only the work of a particular individual woman. Although the Regulations do not permit 'class actions' in the American sense of an individual claimant suing on behalf of an entire group of similarly situated women, it is quite likely that there will be separate complaints filed by many women doing a given job comparing themselves to the same man or men. This will be particularly probable where a trade union is sponsoring the claim.

Case law under the Equal Pay Act makes clear that it is for the applicant to choose her comparator and not for the Tribunal to select the person with whom the comparison should be made.[6] Fears which have been expressed that 'women may be restricted as to which men they can compare themselves with' for the purposes of an equal value claim if they are employed on 'like work' with other men[7] seem groundless. The notion that a woman could be precluded from claiming equal pay with a particular man simply because she is already receiving equal pay with another man goes against all established principles of equal pay and discrimination law.

Even more important is the seeming absence of restrictions on the number of comparators with whom a given complainant can compare herself. The suggestion that the use of the singular in Rule 7A(2)(d), which requires the Tribunal to identify for the independent expert 'the person with reference to whose work the question arises', means that only one comparison can be made,[8] appears ill-founded. Even if such a restricted reading were to be given to the Rules, it could be circumvented by the woman simultaneously filing a separate originating application with respect to each comparison. Provided the comparisons were not manifestly unreasonable, it is submitted that such a course is not only possible, it is advisable from the woman's standpoint. It makes sense for a woman who regards her work as undervalued to compare herself to a range of more highly paid men, each doing different kinds of work.[9]

The Industrial Tribunals (Rules of Procedure)[10] give guidance to the employer faced with multiple claims or multiple comparisons. He should apply to the Tribunal for the complaints to be consolidated and heard together. Rule 15 provides:

> Where there are pending before the industrial tribunals two or more originating applications, then, if at any time upon the application of a party or of its own motion it appears to a tribunal that
>
> (a) some common question of law or fact arises in both or all the originating applications, or
>
> (b) the relief claimed therein is in respect of or arises out of the same set of facts, or
>
> (c) for some other reason it is desirable to make an order under this Rule, the tribunal may order that some (as specified in the order) or all of the originating applications shall be considered together, and may give such consequential directions as may be necessary.

THE MEANING OF 'EQUAL'

The advisability, from the complainant's standpoint, of making more than one comparison is highlighted by the ambiguity which surrounds the meaning of 'equal' in the phrase 'equal value': does equal value, for the purposes of the statute, mean equal or greater value? If a woman, who is paid less than a man, is found to be employed on work which is of greater value than that of a man, will her complaint succeed?

Clearly the spirit of the Regulations, as well as the EEC Equal Pay Directive on which it is based, is that women should be entitled to equal pay if their job is worth at least as much or more than their higher-paid male comparator. However, it is by no means assured that the independent expert and the Industrial Tribunals will approach the problem in this way. A somewhat analogous question arose under the like work sections of the Equal Pay Act in the case of *Waddington v. Leicester Council for Voluntary Services*,[11] where Mrs Waddington complained that she was paid less than her male subordinate. The EAT held that the greater responsibility and control in Mrs Waddington's job were capable of being differences of practical importance between the two jobs so that Mrs Waddington and her higher-paid subordinate were not employed on like work.

If this precedent is followed in the very different context of equal pay for work of equal value claims, it could create chaos. Imagine the case of a woman paid £10 a week less than a man who claims that her work is of equal value. The employer (for the sake of argument) admits that the reason she is paid less is because she is a woman. The Industrial Tribunal sends in the independent expert and he reports that in his view the woman's job is of greater value than the man's. The Tribunal thereupon dismisses the claim because the two jobs are not of equal value. If such is the way in which the law is interpreted, we can envisage the grotesque prospect of women trying to persuade the independent expert that their work is of less value than the expert thinks!

It is submitted that the differences in statutory language between the like work test and the equal value test make the approach of *Waddington* distinguishable and not applicable to equal value claims. The test in s.1(4) is predicated upon there being a sufficient similarity of tasks. The test is one of like work, not equal work. If that similarity does not exist and the work is different, s.1(4) provides no basis for a claim, whether or not the woman has been unfairly treated. The same constraints do not apply to equal pay for work of equal value, since there does not have to be any similarity in tasks to found a claim, just equivalent value.

Nevertheless, it should be pointed out that the Government rejected the suggestion that the language of the Regulations should make it clear that a claim could succeed if the work is of equal or greater value. It follows that unless and until the courts decide that equal means equal or greater, a well-advised complainant will make multiple comparisons if only to ensure that she has not picked a male comparator whose work will be found to be of less value than hers.

NOTES

1. S.1(2)(c).
2. [1977] IRLR 403.
3. See *Barley and others v. Amey Roadstone Corporation Ltd* [1977] IRLR 299 EAT.
4. [1977] IRLR 167.
5. S.6(1A)(b) of the Equal Pay Act excludes from the Act's scope 'terms related to death or retirement'. This means that claims based on work of equal value cannot currently be brought with respect to differences in pension benefits or retirement ages, what has been termed 'equal status' in pension schemes. Although s.6(1A)(a) provides an exception to the exclusion by specifying that an equality clause 'shall operate in relation to terms relating to membership of an occupational pension scheme (within the meaning of the Social Security Pensions Act 1975) so far as those terms relate to any matter in respect of which the scheme has to conform with the equal access requirements of Part IV of that Act', in practice this is of little significance for equal pay purposes. The provisions of the Social Security Pensions Act (s.53) permit differentiation in access according to the nature of employment or any other criterion 'so long as the rule does not provide for the discretion to be exercised in any discriminatory manner as between men and women'.
6. *Ainsworth v. Glass Tubes & Components Ltd* [1977] IRLR 74 EAT.
7. Linda Clarke ('Proposed Amendments to the Equal Pay Act 1970 – II', *New Law Journal*, 23 December, 1983) mounts an argument

expressing this concern on the basis that the Regulations provide that an equal value claim can be made only if the work being compared does not fall within the definitions of like work or work rated as equivalent. She suggests that:

> This could be interpreted as preventing a woman from claiming that her work is of equal value to that of a better paid man, in situations where another man is doing "like work" to her, and is paid perhaps slightly more than she is, or has other more advantageous contractual terms . . . If there is a man doing the work, or work of a broadly similar nature, or a man whose work has been rated as equivalent, then it is possible that the Tribunal will only allow a woman to claim parity with *this* man, rather than another man whom she believes is doing work "of equal value" and is significantly better paid than she is.

In fact, a woman is better off making a like work claim than an equal value claim if she can with respect to the same man, since the employer's defence is narrower and the full back pay provisions will apply immediately.

8. This is suggested by Richard Townshend-Smith ('The Equal Pay (Amendment) Regulations 1983, *The Modern Law Review*, vol. 47, no. 2, March 1984). He goes on to argue that 'this means that the burden of choosing the correct comparator is very significant'.
9. Because of the importance of this point, those advising women should follow the early Industrial Tribunal case law to determine whether multiple comparisons can be made under a single originating application or whether separate originating applications are required for each comparison.
10. S.I. 1980 No. 884.
11. [1977] IRLR 32.

5 Bringing a Complaint

This chapter looks at the mechanics for bringing a claim for equal pay for work of equal value.

ORIGINATING APPLICATION AND NOTICE OF APPEARANCE

In order to institute a claim for equal pay for work of equal value, an applicant must present an originating application to the Industrial Tribunals, setting out her name and address, the name and address of the employer and the grounds, with particulars thereof, on which the applicant seeks relief.

Claims under the Equal Pay Act, including equal value claims, can be brought by existing employees and by former employees, provided in the latter case that the applicant was employed in the employment in question within a six month period preceding the date of the application – s.2(4).

Where an applicant wishes to make multiple comparisons – e.g. she is a clerical supervisor and she wants to compare the value of her work to a range of more highly paid men, each performing different work, say shop-floor foremen, lorry drivers, lab technicians and computer programmers – it may be advisable to file a *separate* originating application in respect of each comparison.

There is nothing in the Rules of Procedure requiring the applicant to designate her comparator or comparators by name in the originating application. As a matter of practice, however, some information, such as the job title of the male comparators, ought to be provided in the originating application since, unless this is done, the Secretary of the Tribunals is likely to ask for further particulars of the complaint to be furnished. At some point in the proceedings, the comparator must be identified by name, as this must be included in the requirement given to the independent expert. If the claim gets that far, the name of the comparator can be ascertained through the normal interlocutory proceedings.

The Secretary of the Tribunals will send a copy of the originating application to the employer, who has fourteen days to enter an appearance by presenting a written 'notice of appearance' to the Secretary. If the employer intends to resist the claim, the notice of appearance should set out sufficient particulars to show the grounds upon which he proposes to do so. In most cases, the employer will wish to plead in the alternative – he will deny that the applicant is employed on work of equal value with her comparator, but will wish to argue that if she is employed on work of equal value, the variation in pay is not sex-based.

CONCILIATION

As with other types of complaints to an Industrial Tribunal, a copy of a complaint relating to equal pay for work of equal value will be sent to an ACAS conciliation officer.

In keeping with the overall intention of minimising the number of complaints to be referred to an independent expert, Rule 12(2A) of the amended Rules of Procedure introduces a further and novel conciliation provision – the invitation for an adjournment. According to the Rule, 'in a case involving an equal value claim the tribunal shall, before proceeding to hear the parties on the claim, invite them to apply for an adjournment for the purpose of seeking to reach a settlement of the claim and shall, if both or all the parties agree to such a course, grant an adjournment for that purpose'.

PREPARATIONS

If conciliation fails, the Industrial Tribunal must conduct a preliminary hearing on whether the complaint should be dismissed without further investigation by reason of there being 'no reasonable grounds for determining that the work is of equal value'.

Before that preliminary hearing takes place, however, there are likely to be exchanges of information between the parties, the extent of which may depend largely on the approach the Tribunals adopt at the screening stage.

It is a general principle of British law that a party to proceedings has a right to know reasonable details of the nature of the other side's case before the hearing. This principle is embodied in Rule 4(1)(i) of the Rules of Procedure, which empowers a Tribunal to 'require a party to furnish in writing to the person specified by the tribunal further particulars of the grounds on which he or it relies and of any facts and contentions relevant thereto'. The right to further particulars is supplemented by a right to discovery or inspection of documents. The criteria for whether discovery or inspection should be ordered are, as laid down in the County Court Rules, that it is necessary for disposing fairly of the proceedings. Either party can apply to the Industrial Tribunal for an order requiring further particulars and/or discovery.

In an equal value claim, the employer will want to know before the preliminary hearing the precise grounds the applicant has for thinking she is employed on work of equal value with her male comparator.

Given the nature of the claim, however, it is the applicant in an equal value case who will normally have the greater informational needs – and the more rigorous the Tribunals are at the screening stage, the more information she is going to want so as to be able to demonstrate that her case is based on reasonable grounds.

To illustrate the potential scope of the information which employers may have to reveal, let us take the example of the female clerical supervisor comparing the value of her work to that of a male craftsman. This is a typical case cutting across existing pay grades and negotiating groups. In order to argue that there are reasonable grounds for her case, she must first ascertain whether her comparator is more highly paid or is treated more favourably in other ways. This means she will want details of what the man is paid, including his package of contractual fringe benefits. Secondly, she must know details of the man's work so that she can make her case that her work is equal. This means she will want to be provided with details such as his contract of employment and his job description. The applicant must also show reasonable grounds for believing that her work has been undervalued in comparison with the man's. In order to do so, she must know (if she does not know already) how her own work is valued. More importantly, she will want to know the basis of the valuation of her male comparator's work.[1]

There is a real possibility, therefore, that the new Regulations will prove a serious threat to confidentiality in payment systems. Unlike discrimination cases involving selection or promotion, where on the facts it may not be necessary to reveal personal information about another employee in order to determine whether there has been unlawful discrimination, an equal value case – by definition – is a comparison between the value of the work done (and possibly the personal characteristics) of two employees. Adopting the principles set out by the House of Lords in *Science Research Council v. Nasse* and *Vyas v. Leyland Cars*,[2] it is difficult to see how equal value proceedings can be fairly disposed of without revealing information that may hitherto have been regarded by the employer as confidential.

THE SCREENING HEARING

The Regulations confer on Industrial Tribunals the duty to conduct a preliminary hearing to determine whether an equal value complaint should be dismissed without further investigation if it is held that there are 'no reasonable grounds for determining that the work is of equal value'. The provision for such a screening hearing is an unprecedented impediment. The Tribunal already has powers to strike out a claim at any stage of the proceedings on grounds that it is 'frivolous or vexatious'.[3] In addition, the Tribunal can issue a warning as to costs following a pre-hearing assessment on the application of either party.[4]

Both the language and the substance of the Regulations requiring a preliminary hearing have been subjected to heavy criticism.[5] The amended s.2A(1) states:

> Where on a complaint or reference made to an industrial tribunal under section 2 above a dispute arises as to whether any work is of equal value as mentioned in section 1(2)(c) above the tribunal shall not determine that question unless –
>
> (a) it is satisfied that there are no reasonable grounds for determining that the work is of equal value as so mentioned; or
>
> (b) it has required a member of the panel of independent experts to prepare a report with respect to that question and has received that report.

These words, if they have any meaning at all, direct the Tribunal to decide first whether there are no reasonable grounds for thinking that the two jobs being compared are of equal value. If it decides that there are no reasonable grounds, it must 'determine' the case then and there by dismissing the complaint. But if it concludes that there are reasonable grounds for thinking that the work is of equal value (or, to put it more accurately, if it cannot be held that there are no reasonable grounds), then the question of whether the work is of equal value cannot be decided until the Tribunal has received the report of the independent expert.

The Government's intention is to save the expense of an expert's report where the claim is clearly without merit. Lord Gowrie, the Government spokesman in the House of Lords' debate on the Regulations, stated: 'The new power to throw out the case is in recognition of the fact that to allow a hopeless case to continue will be expensive and time-consuming for all concerned. I stress that it is only the hopeless case that will be excluded by this regulation. If there is any doubt, it must be resolved in the applicant's favour and the case will proceed in the normal way.'[6]

Whether it is only the 'hopeless' case that is barred at this stage must remain to be seen. It should be stressed, however, that the provision is directory upon the Tribunal. It is not up to the employer to raise the question; the Tribunal must answer it one way or the other. But the Tribunal can only answer the question by hearing evidence and argument from the parties. How much evidence and argument will be required depends upon how the Tribunals see their role at this stage. Note the paradox that the more thorough the screen, the more evidence and argument will be necessary at this stage, the less thorough the screen and the more cases that go through to the expert, the simpler the preliminary hearing will be.

WORK PREVIOUSLY EVALUATED

The Regulations build in a further screen at the preliminary stage. If the jobs being compared have already been given different values under a job evaluation study, the claim cannot proceed provided that there are not reasonable grounds for determining that the job evaluation system discriminated on grounds of sex.

The proviso permitting claims to go forward to the independent expert, if a job evaluation is held to be discriminatory, was a significant concession by the Government in response to representations. The Government originally proposed simply to block claims where work had previously been rated as not equivalent.[7]

As we have seen, the question of whether job evaluation schemes discriminate directly or indirectly on grounds of sex is central to the thesis that women's work is undervalued because it is performed by women. In the long term, the provision for judicial scrutiny of whether a job evaluation scheme is discriminatory may prove to be an aspect of the Regulations of the greatest practical importance for pay determination. Because of this, we deal separately with both the legal and personnel implications of whether a job evaluation scheme discriminates in the next chapter. Suffice it to say at this stage that two general issues are posed: first, have the jobs in question been given different values under a study within the statutory definition? Secondly, if so, can the Tribunal determine that there are no reasonable grounds for finding that the evaluation was made on a system which discriminates on grounds of sex? If the Tribunal is satisfied as to both these questions, the claim will be dismissed. If the Tribunal finds either of these conditions are not satisfied, the claim will normally proceed to the next stage, the reference to the independent expert.

THE EMPLOYER'S DEFENCE: FIRST OPPORTUNITY

Before the Tribunal commissions a report from the independent expert, Rule 8(2E) of the Procedural Regulations gives the employer the opportunity to ask the Tribunal to hear arguments as to whether any variation in pay, even if the work is found to be of equal value, falls within the defence provided by the amended s.1(3) – that the variation was 'genuinely due to a material factor which is not the difference of sex'.

Where the employer has a defence which stands a reasonable prospect of success, it will make sense from the standpoint of costs and convenience for him to apply to the Tribunal for his defence to be heard before the expert begins investigation. Clearly, this will be the case where the defence is straightforward – for example, where the pay differential results entirely from differences in service and has nothing to do with sex. Equally, it may be thought right to argue the defence under s.1(3) where complex legal issues are involved before referring the case to the expert.[8] Whichever way it is approached, one of the questions – whether the work is of equal value or whether the employer has a defence – can make the other question academic. It is submitted that the uncertainty engendered whilst the expert is preparing his report tips the balance on the side of disposing of the legal issues first where possible.

That the Regulations offer the employer two opportunities to put forward a defence under s.1(3) – before the reference to the independent expert and at the resumed hearing if the Tribunal finds, after receiving the expert's report, that the work is of equal value – was criticised by the Labour Party in the House of Lords, amongst others, as offering 'two bites of the cherry'.[9] In the debate on the motion to annul the Procedural Regulations, Lord Gowrie responded by claiming that the Regulations have 'been so worded as to limit the initial consideration of a material factor defence to clear-cut cases where it is obvious that claims cannot succeed'.[10] This may be the aspiration, but there is nothing in the language of the Regulations restricting consideration of the defence at this preliminary stage to 'clear-cut cases'. On the contrary, the matter is left entirely within the discretion of the Industrial Tribunal.

Where Lord Gowrie was on stronger ground was in asserting that the opportunity to put forward a defence both before and after the expert's report does not really provide the employer with 'two bites of the cherry'. He claimed that 'The fact that an employer can also put forward a material factor defence after an expert has reported will not mean that an employer will be able to deploy the same arguments twice with any hope of success. An employer rehearsing a rejected argument without fresh grounds or evidence would naturally be likely to get short shrift from a Tribunal, and he could even in those cases incur the payment of costs.'[11] Although Regulation 8(2E) does provide that where the Tribunal has heard evidence on the employer's defence prior to requiring the expert to prepare a report, 'it shall be without prejudice to further consideration of that issue after the Tribunal has received the report',[12] it is submitted that the reference to 'that issue' means the general question of whether the employer has a defence under s.1(3). Having put forward unsuccessfully a specific defence at the preliminary stage, the principle of issue estoppel would seem to preclude the employer arguing the same – though not a different – defence when the expert reported, even if he had fresh evidence to support his argument.

Although chronologically, in many cases the employer's defence under s.1(3) will be argued before the case has been referred to the independent expert, logically whether the employer has a defence to unequal pay is an issue to be considered after it has been found that the work is of equal value. Therefore, we deal with the substantive questions relating to the employer's defence in a separate chapter, following consideration of the work of the independent expert.

NOTES

1. In this context, it may be interesting to look at a parallel American experience. Following the decision in 1981 by the United States Supreme Court in *County of Washington v. Gunther* (25 FEP Cases 1521) that sex-based wage discrimination claims could be brought under Title VII of the Civil Rights Act 1964 and did not have to satisfy the equal work standards of the Equal Pay Act 1963, the US Equal Employment Opportunity Commission, which has enforcement powers under Title VII, issued guidelines for its specialists in the field on the information they should obtain to identify sex-based wage discrimination. According to the notice, issued on 25 August 1981, the following information should be obtained:

   1. A breakdown of the employer's work force by sex in terms of job classifications, assignments, and duties;
   2. Written detailed job descriptions . . .;
   3. Wage schedules broken down in terms of sex showing job classifications, assignments, and duties;
   4. Any documents which show the history of the employer's wage schedules such as collective bargaining agreements . . .
   5. All employer justification of, or defences to, the sex-based wage disparity;
   6. If a job evaluation system is the basis for the sex-based wage disparity . . . copies of the evaluation and, if available, an analysis of its purpose and operation;
   7. If market wage rate is the basis for the sex-based wage disparity, determine the underlying factors relied upon by the employer and the methods the employer used to determine the market wage rate;
   8. If union collective bargaining agreements are the basis for the sex-based wage disparity . . . obtain copies of those agreements; and
   9. Any evidence which shows that the employer or the employer and the union have established and maintained sex-segregated job categories.

2. [1979] IRLR 465.
3. Rule 12(2)(e).
4. Rule 6(2). It is possible, in theory, for a party to an equal value dispute to ask for a pre-hearing assessment, but in practice the existence of the screening hearing renders the pre-hearing assessment unnecessary.
5. Whether the language of this part of the Regulations is defective excited editorial comment and correspondence in the *New Law*

Journal. Some, such as the NLJ's editor, suggested that the use of a double negative in the subsection (the tribunal 'shall not determine that question unless . . . it is satisfied that there are no reasonable grounds for determining that the work is of equal value') in formal logic means 'if there are reasonable grounds for making a determination, the tribunal shall not make a determination' ('Legislating Nonsense', NLJ, 5 August, 1983 and 'Sense and Nonsense in the Law, NIJ, 14 October, 1983). Others, such as the present author (NIJ, 26 August, 1983) argued that the Regulation, although obscurely worded was not defective in this respect.

6. *Hansard*, House of Lords, 5.12.83, col. 524.
7. Consultative Draft Statutory Instrument, February 1983. The thrust of the European Court's decision was to require the Equal Pay Act to be amended so as to permit claims for equal pay for work of equal value where work has not been evaluated at all. However, it was pointed out to the Government that simply to bar claims where work had been evaluated as unequal would open the door to abuses in that discriminatory schemes could be installed so as to preclude the exercise of the new statutory right.
8. McCrudden ('Equal Pay for Work of Equal Value', *The Industrial Law Journal*, vol. 13, no. 1, March, 1984) takes the opposite view: 'Given the potential complexities raised by the defence, sensible tribunals will often prefer to leave the issue until after receiving the expert's report.'
9. *Hansard*, House of Lords, 12.12.83.
10. *Hansard*, House of Lords, 1.2.84, col. 743.
11. Ibid.
12. Strictly construed, the Regulations do not appear to empower the Tribunal to dismiss the claim in such circumstances before receiving the report of the independent expert. As Brian Napier has pointed out ('Equal Pay For Work Of Equal Value', *Scots Law Times*, 10 February, 1984), 'it is probable that the applicant can still insist on her claim going forward, notwithstanding an adverse finding, since any other conclusion would involve a reading of Rule 8(2E) which would make it ultra vires'. However, as Napier also suggests, in practice such a course of conduct seems improbable since it would be likely to render the applicant liable for an award of costs.'

6 Discriminatory Job Evaluation and the Law

The European Court held that the United Kingdom was not in compliance with EEC law because the 1970 Equal Pay Act provided no right to equal pay for work of equal value where the jobs in question had not been evaluated. In order to comply with the Court's decision, the Government introduced amending Regulations to permit claims to be brought for equal pay for work of equal value. S.1(5) of the 1970 Act already provided a right to equal pay where work has been rated as equivalent (or of equal value) under a job evaluation scheme. The Government's original intention was merely to provide recourse where the jobs being compared had not been the subject of job evaluation. This had the merit of precluding applicants from seeking to upset the outcome of job evaluation schemes, which are frequently the result of difficult negotiations. For this reason, the Regulations in their original form barred claims where the jobs in question had been evaluated as unequal.

The problem with stopping there was that s.1(5) provides no safeguard against a discriminatory evaluation except in the limited circumstances of an overtly discriminatory scheme setting different rates for men and women on the same demand. This raised the prospect of an employer being able to rely on a job evaluation scheme to avoid liability under the Regulations even if such a scheme discriminated on grounds of sex. As well as producing an anomaly, it is likely that this would have entailed a continuing breach of the EEC Directive.[1] In order to avoid this, the Government altered its proposals to further provide that the bar on claims where work has already been evaluated as unequal would only operate if the evaluation did not discriminate on grounds of sex.

The Regulations, therefore, allow an applicant to challenge an evaluation by the employer that her job was of less value than that of her male comparator on grounds that the evaluation was discriminatory. The significance of a finding that a scheme may discriminate on grounds of sex hardly needs emphasising.[2] Its importance lies less in the immediate outcome of such a finding, which is simply to permit the claim for equal pay for work of equal value to proceed to the next stage, than in its repercussions for the pay structure and system of pay determination in the organisation in question. Although the legal consequences are uncertain, from a personnel standpoint it is doubtful whether an employer could continue to operate a job evaluation system that has been declared to be suspect by an Industrial Tribunal.

Because of its consequences, we might have expected the sections of the Regulations which deal with discriminatory job evaluation schemes to be especially carefully and clearly drafted. Instead, as we shall see, there are parts of the relevant sections which hardly make sense at all.

This chapter, within the constraints imposed by the drafting of the Regulations, considers the issues which will have to be determined when an equal value claim is made to the Tribunal in circumstances where the employer's evaluation has determined that the jobs being compared are not of equal value.

HAVE THE JOBS BEEN EVALUATED AS UNEQUAL?

The first issue which the Tribunal has to determine is whether or not there is a prima facie bar to the claim. The first limb of new s.2A(2) states: 'Without prejudice to the generality of paragraph (a) of subsection (1) above, there shall be taken, for the purposes of that paragraph, to be no reasonable grounds for determining that the work of a woman is of equal value as mentioned in s.1(2)(c) above if

(a) that work and the work of the man in question have been given different values on a study such as is mentioned in section 1(5) above.'

Therefore, the Tribunal must determine whether the two jobs have been rated as not equivalent by a study within the meaning of s.1(5).[3] S.1(5) provides:

> A woman is to be regarded as employed on work rated as equivalent with that of any men if, but only if, her job and their job have been given an equal value, in terms of the demand made on a worker under various headings (for instance effort, skill, decision), on a study undertaken with a view to evaluating in those terms the jobs to be done by all or any of the employees in an undertaking or group of undertakings, or would have been given an equal value but for the evaluation being made on a system setting different values for men and women on the same demand under any heading.

It will be noted that nowhere in the definition is the phrase 'job evaluation' used, though this is clearly what the draftsman of the 1970 Act had in mind. The definition used is rather more precise – a study evaluating 'the demand made on a worker under various headings (for instance effort, skill, decision)'. This distinction may be important. The rubric 'job evaluation' is applied to any systematic procedure for analysing a group of jobs and determining their relative worth. Within this wide spectrum, a distinction is commonly drawn between methods which compare and order each job as a whole and methods which analyse the characteristics of each job. The first category, which is termed 'non-analytical', includes methods such as job ranking, job classification, and paired comparisons. This is less common than 'analytic' methods such as points rating,[4] but it is still employed by a substantial number of organisations, both for manual and non-manual staff.

Non-analytic methods of job evaluation are inherently more subjective than analytic methods since the outcome is entirely a matter of the opinion of the evaluator. This high degree of subjectivity makes non-analytic systems of job evaluation especially prone to sex discrimination.[5]

It might be that an applicant could prove that an evaluation produced by a non-analytic method was sexually discriminatory. But this is unlikely to be necessary. In order to fall within s.1(5), and therefore s.2A(2)(a), what must be evaluated is 'the demand made on a worker under various headings (for instance effort, skill, decision)'. Evaluators using non-analytic methods clearly must have some frame of reference for ordering jobs and doubtless it will often include effort, skill and decision. But, by definition, non-analytic methods do not evaluate the demand made on a worker under these various headings. Therefore, it is submitted that on a correct reading of the Regulations, that two jobs have been judged unequal under a non-analytic method of evaluation will not bar a claim for equal pay for work of equal value.[6]

The question of whether non-analytic methods meet the requirements of s.1(5) is not an issue which has been considered in terms at appellate level under the 1970 Act. However, case law under the Equal Pay Act has set out the principle that s.1(5) applies only to a 'valid' job evaluation and an absence of subjectivity has been a leading criterion for validity in the eyes of the courts. In *Eaton Ltd* v. *Nuttall*,[7] the EAT took the view that a 'valid' evaluation must

> mean a study satisfying the test of being thorough in analysis and capable of impartial application. It should be possible by applying the study to arrive at the position of a particular employee at a particular point in a particular salary grade without taking other matters into account except those unconnected with the nature of the work. It will be in order to take into account such matters as merit or seniority, etc., but any matters concerning the work (e.g. responsibility) one would expect to find taken care of in the evaluation study. One which does not satisfy that test, and requires the management to make a subjective judgement concerning the nature of the work before the employee can be fitted into the appropriate place in the appropriate salary grade, would seem to us not to be a valid study for the purpose of sub-section (5).

And in *England* v. *The London Borough of Bromley*,[8] the EAT added that the study 'should be complete and objective and by its application enable all factors of importance in relation to the work to be taken into account, making it unnecessary for the employers to make subjective judgements upon the work content'.

Were these dicta to be applied to the letter, it is doubtful whether any job evaluation scheme would meet the test proposed since it is necessary in even the most rigorously analytic scheme for 'subjective judgements upon the work content' to be made. Nonetheless, the spirit underlying the EAT's views suggests that the courts will carefully scrutinise particular systems of evaluation to ensure that they meet the minimum standards of relative objectivity implied by s.1(5).

Under s.1(5) of the 1970 Act, a claimant could only succeed if she could show that her work had been rated as equivalent to that of a man. Under the Equal Value Regulations, the claimant is seeking precisely the opposite finding, that the work has not been rated as equivalent. This raises the same temporal question which has been considered by the courts under the 1970 Act – when can it be said that work has been rated as equivalent? Given that there are a number of steps to be taken before a decision to conduct a job evaluation results in an operative change to a pay structure, the issue here is at what point along this continuum should it be held that the work has been rated as equivalent or not equivalent for the purposes of the Act? In *O'Brien and others* v. *Sim-Chem Ltd*,[9] the House of Lords ruled that it is sufficient that the job evaluation study has been undertaken and has resulted in a conclusion evaluating the two jobs in question so that a comparison can be made. It is not necessary for the results of the job evaluation scheme to have been put into practice.

In the subsequent case of *Arnold* v. *Beecham Group Ltd*,[10] the EAT limited this principle by adding the caveat that the results of the study when completed must be accepted by the parties concerned. According to the EAT, before s.1(5) can be applied there must be a completed job evaluation study and 'there is no complete job evaluation study falling within s.1(5) of the Act unless and until it has been accepted or adopted by employers and employees as regulating their relationship'. The EAT distinguished *O'Brien* v. *Sim-Chem* on grounds that in that case the job evaluation study had been agreed and all that remained was to put money to the figures. 'It is perfectly possible to accept the validity of a study at a stage substantially before it is implemented by being used as the basis of the payment of remuneration. It is not the stage of implementing the study which makes it complete: it is the stage at which it is accepted as a study.'

It has been suggested that 'on a narrow reading of the proposed s.2A(2)(a) of the Equal Pay Act 1970, an employer could argue that once a JES has been carried out which gives the work of a woman and of the man in question different values, then she is precluded from claiming that their work is of equal value, even though the employer has refused to accept or implement the JES'.[11] Such an interpretation seems highly improbable since it would entail permitting the same employer who has used the non-acceptance of the scheme as a shield to block claims under s.1(5) also to use the scheme which he has not accepted as a sword to block claims under s.2A(2)(a).

Nonetheless, *Arnold* v. *Beecham Group* does pose real problems for the interpretation of the new Regulations. The EAT's decision left unanswered the consequences if the employer is unhappy with the scheme but the union is not, or vice versa; or if the employer and some unions accept the study but other unions do not; or, for that matter, if the women do not accept the study's validity. The spirit of *Arnold* is that in any of these circumstances the study will not be regarded as complete so that equal value claims will not be barred. Whether that is how the language of the Regulations will be interpreted remains to be seen.

NO REASONABLE GROUNDS

That two jobs have been rated as unequal by an employer's evaluation is not sufficient in itself to bar an equal value complaint. S.2A(2)(b) specifies that in such circumstances a claim will only be precluded where, in addition, 'there are no reasonable grounds for determining that the evaluation contained in the study was (within the meaning of subsection

(3) below) made on a system which discriminates on grounds of sex'.

Whether a job evaluation scheme discriminates on grounds of sex, therefore, is to be determined in accordance with the language of new s.2A(3). Before considering this definition, it is worth examining the standard of proof set out in s.2A(2)(b). By its reference to 'no reasonable grounds', this parallels the phraseology in s.2A(1)(a) where the Tribunal is instructed to bar the claim if it is satisfied 'that there are no reasonable grounds for determining that the work is of equal value'. As we saw above, the Government's spokesman in the House of Lords, Lord Gowrie, was at pains to explain that 'it is only the hopeless case that will be excluded by this Regulation. If there is any doubt, it must be resolved in the applicant's favour and the case will proceed in the normal way'. This clearly implies a very severe standard of proof for determining that there are no reasonable grounds (or, to put it the other way round at the expense of strict accuracy, it should be relatively easy to demonstrate that there were reasonable grounds).

Identical language is used in s.2A(2)(b), in a context where the Regulations would have made equal sense if the phrase 'there are no reasonable grounds for determining that' had been omitted altogether.

The result is that the Tribunal does not have to find in terms that the scheme actually discriminates. There is an evidential burden of proof on the employer to show that (a) a job evaluation scheme exists, (b) the scheme meets the requirements of s.1(5) and (c) the jobs in question have been evaluated as unequal under the scheme. The evidential burden will then shift to the applicant to show some evidence that the evaluation was discriminatory – as defined in s.2A(3). How difficult this will be as a matter of practice is discussed in the subsequent section. But the use of the words 'there are no reasonable grounds' suggest that the standard that is required is far less onerous than if the applicant had to persuade the Tribunal on a balance of probabilities that there was discrimination.

A low standard of proof is all very well when the sole issue in the case is whether the claim should be thrown out at the preliminary stage because it is hopeless – s.2A(1)(a). Altogether different considerations apply when, as a necessary step in determining that the claim should be allowed to proceed, the Tribunal must make some sort of determination on whether the job evaluation system discriminates on grounds of sex. Whatever its virtues in allowing claims to go forward, from a personnel and industrial relations standpoint such a procedure is patently absurd. Whenever a claim is allowed through the screen of s.2A(2)(b), the organisation in question will be left with an aspersion cast on the bona fides of its payment system and it may be unable to determine whether the Tribunal would have reached the same conclusion as to whether the job evaluation scheme discriminates were it approaching the matter on the ordinary test of the balance of probabilities. That such an outcome is even possible suggests a remarkable lack of sensitivity on the part of those responsible for these Regulations. Whether the scheme is discriminatory will not be resolved by the independent expert to whom the claim is then referred.[12] The expert is merely asked to determine whether two jobs evaluated under the scheme are of equal value. This is a different question. He may conclude that the jobs were wrongly evaluated as unequal, but that does not resolve the issue of whether the reasons for their unequal evaluation were discriminatory. He may conclude that they were correctly evaluated as unequal for reasons specific to the particular jobs, but it does not necessarily follow that that refutes an inference that the scheme itself is discriminatory. Thus, a finding by the independent expert that the work is of unequal value cannot be regarded as vindicating the non-discriminatory nature of the job evaluation system.[13]

VALUES NOT JUSTIFIABLE

The problems posed by the use of the phrase 'no reasonable grounds' pale by comparison with that portended by the actual definition of discriminatory job evaluation in s.2A(3). This provides: 'An evaluation contained in a study such as is mentioned in s.1(5) above is made on a system which discriminates on grounds of sex where a difference, or coincidence, between values set by that system on different demands under the same or different headings is not justifiable irrespective of the sex of the person on whom those demands are made.'

The statutory language, as we shall see, is capable of embracing job evaluation schemes which discriminate either directly or indirectly. Doubtless, this is the Government's intention. The difficulty is that the ordinary meaning of the language used is to permit a job evaluation to be challenged on grounds that its outcome is not 'justifiable' regardless of whether or not the scheme discriminates on grounds of sex. In marked contrast to the definition of discrimination under the Sex Discrimination Act, there is no explicit requirement either to show that the reason for the less favourable treatment is the sex of the person concerned or that the values used by the system have a disproportionate impact upon women. This becomes clear when the clause is examined limb by limb:

An evaluation contained in a study such as is mentioned in s.1(5) above: the work has been evaluated under a study which measures effort, skill, decision.

is made on a system which discriminates on grounds of sex: a declaratory statement.

where a difference, or coincidence, between values set by that system on different demands: i.e. the evaluation scheme sets a value (such as by awarding points) on various demands (e.g. strength, dexterity) and those values may either coincide or be different.

under the same or different headings: i.e. both strength and dexterity may be measured under 'effort' or strength may come under 'effort' and dexterity under 'skill'.

is not justifiable: the determinative consideration.

irrespective of the sex of the person on whom those demands are made: the difference or coincidence in values cannot be justified by reference to the sex of the workers concerned.

In short, a job evaluation scheme discriminates on grounds of sex where its results are not 'justifiable'.

Writing in the *New Law Journal* last year,[14] I suggested that these provisions were defective because they do not incorporate any standard for determining whether the job evaluation scheme discriminates on grounds of sex. The words 'irrespective of the sex of the person on whom those demands are made' provide no assistance. They merely import into the test of justifiability a constraint that the purported justification for the difference cannot have regard to the sex of the person concerned. In *Mandla* v. *Lee*,[15] the House of Lords, construing the directly parallel provisions of the Race Relations Act, decided that the words justifiable 'irrespective of the colour', etc., of the person to whom a condition is applied meant that it must be justifiable 'without regard to' the ethnic origin of that person. In that case, a 'no turban' rule could not be justified on grounds that the turban was objectionable because it was a manifestation of the complainant's ethnic origins, since such a justification had regard to ethnic origins. Applying that construction to the equal value Regulations, the words simply mean that the employer cannot attempt to justify differences in, for example, factor weightings on grounds of purported differences between men and women.

Without reading words into the statutory definition, therefore, in theory it would be possible for a woman whose work had been evaluated as of less value than that of a man to challenge the scheme, merely because she thinks that the evaluation is not justifiable, and the employer would be required to justify the evaluation.

This is precisely the interpretation which has been put on the Regulations by other early commentators without demur. Thus Anthony Lester claims that 'a woman may challenge a job evaluation study where there is . . . a difference in the values set for the woman's work and the man's work'.[16] Lester dresses up this concept as 'disparate adverse treatment', but in plain English it means nothing more than that the woman is paid less than the man. *Industrial Relations Legal Information Bulletin* points out that 'a woman may argue that instead of manual dexterity being given fewer points than physical strength, it should have been given the same . . . It is not necessary to show that the alleged defect has a disparate impact upon women – that seems to be assumed from the JES having rated the woman's job differently from the man's'.[17] If so, it is an extraordinary assumption.

Under the strict language of the statute, then, an inference of sex discrimination is created merely by the fact that a woman is paid less than a man and the test for whether the evaluation is discriminatory does not necessarily involve any further evidence of direct or indirect discrimination. Nor, for all that appears on the statute book, is it particularly relevant for the employer to show that his evaluation was non-discriminatory. The question is simply whether the difference is 'justifiable'.[18] Job evaluation being an imprecise science, it is not difficult to think of many examples where a Tribunal might regard an evaluation as unjustifiable for reasons which have nothing to do with sex discrimination.

Such a scenario is sufficiently illogical to make it improbable that s.2A(3) will be interpreted in this way. Although the statutory test should have been altered to incorporate a standard of discrimination, it is highly likely that the courts will find some way of giving the words used a purposive construction so as to restrict claims to where evidence is brought, not merely to show that the evaluation resulted in different pay for men and women, but where the evidence suggests an inference that a particular aspect of the evaluation scheme is tainted by sex discrimination. In the next section, therefore, we assume that the Tribunal will be assessing the scheme to make some judgment as to whether it discriminates on grounds of sex within the established legal definitions of discrimination and we look at the legal and evidential tests that may be adopted. Readers should bear in mind that the question of whether an evaluation is discriminatory may also arise in assessing the valuation arrived at by the independent expert. Thus, many of the same tests suggested below for determining whether an employer's scheme is discriminatory may be of use in challenging the independent expert's report.

DISCRIMINATION AND THE PROCESS OF JOB EVALUATION

Job evaluation is a management tool for systematising the subjective judgements that underpin existing pay differentials. It provides a 'rational' system of wage differentials that organisations can understand, explain, defend and administer.

We suggested above that only schemes which analyse job content according to a number of demands or factors will fall within the scope of the Regulations as having the potential to block an equal value claim if the evaluation was not discriminatory. The most popular analytic scheme is points rating. This requires the analysis of each job (or a range of representative 'benchmark' jobs) under a number of predetermined factors or job characteristics.[19]

The factors chosen are termed 'compensable factors' because they are the aspects of the job which the organisation wishes to reward. These factors are then normally weighted to reflect the relative importance the organisation attaches to each particular factor.

It is part of the ethos of job evaluation that the wage structure arrived at should be regarded as 'fair'. Some job evaluation methods, such as job ranking, are nothing more than a hierarchical ordering of jobs on the basis of what is felt fair. But even systems which are more analytic employ perceptions of fairness, either in the choice and mix of factors or as a means of checking the results.

A 'fair' evaluation is usually seen as one which broadly replicates the existing hierarchy of jobs. This is what we would expect; were it not the case, there would be something radically wrong with the previous pay structure. For this reason, when introducing job evaluation, it is common for a company to accept existing wage rates as the criterion of job value and seek to find the factors that will best predict the existing wage differentials. This is sometimes termed 'policy-capturing', because it makes explicit the unarticulated system already being used.

What is regarded as 'fair', however, and what is not sexually discriminatory are not the same. Job evaluation systems, at least until now, have been aimed at providing an acceptable result, not at complying with a legal standard of discrimination. There may be widespread agreement that the jobs women do are 'worth' less than those of men, but this may stem from the socialisation of sexist values. Earlier in this book we suggested that there was considerable reason for thinking that the work women do is undervalued because it is performed by women. To the extent that this proposition is valid and the wage structure undervalues women's jobs, the effect of job evaluation will be to perpetuate the status quo and to institutionalise this undervaluation in a miasma of scientific-looking equations. The process is circular.[20]

The new Regulations, therefore, present acute problems for organisations with job evaluated salary structures. Evaluation schemes will be vulnerable to charges of direct and indirect discrimination, but the price of a scheme which is less discriminatory may well be a scheme which is less acceptable to the majority. If there is a way round this problem, it can only lie with changing attitudes as to what is and what is not fair. From a personnel and industrial relations standpoint, this suggests that employers (and, for that matter, trade unions) would be well advised to consider specific training and communications measures on why it is important that women's work should not be discriminatorily undervalued.

The definition of discrimination in the Sex Discrimination Act incorporates two theories of discrimination: less favourable treatment on grounds of sex and unjustifiable indirect discrimination. S.1(3) of the Equal Pay Act expressly incorporates the concept of less favourable treatment on grounds of sex and, in *Jenkins* v. *Kingsgate No. 2*, the EAT construed the Equal Pay Act as, in effect, incorporating a standard of indirect discrimination. There can be little doubt, therefore, that the reference to a job evaluation scheme that 'discriminates on grounds of sex' in s.2A(2) and 2A(3) relates back to the two definitions of discrimination embodied in s.1 of the Sex Discrimination Act.

There is a detailed discussion of the meaning of the two definitions of discrimination in Chapter 8, in the context of the employer's defence that unequal pay is genuinely due to a material factor other than the difference of sex. Here, we consider the main points in so far as they relate to discriminatory job evaluation. There is one crucial point which we must summarise, however. The distinction between so-called 'direct' and indirect discrimination does not lie in whether the reason put forward by the employer is 'neutral' or whether it is expressly tied to sex. Neutral reasons will invariably be put forward by the employer to explain his conduct. The distinction between the two forms of discrimination lies in whether the neutral reason is genuine, in which case it must be tested for whether it has an unjustifiable disparate impact upon one sex or the other, or whether the neutral reason is a pretext for the real reason lying behind the employer's conduct, the sex of the workers concerned. It follows that any question as to whether the operation of a job evaluation scheme is discriminatory can be tested under both theories of discrimination: if women are disadvantaged by the aspect of the scheme in point, the first question is whether the explanation put forward by the employer is true. Only if that explanation is genuine does the question of whether it is justifiable arise.

From this reasoning, a further principle follows: a job evaluation scheme cannot be held to discriminate on grounds of sex unless one sex is disproportionately over-represented in the particular job under scrutiny. This is a simple point, but one which it is important not to lose sight of in the ensuing discussion. Where a post is held relatively equally by men and women, that an element in the job evaluation disadvantages a woman complainant cannot be held to be on grounds of her sex, since men will be equally disadvantaged by that element. Nor will it be possible to show that the aspect complained of had a disproportionate impact upon women so as to make it potentially indirectly discriminatory.

DISPARATE TREATMENT

S.1(1)(a) of the Sex Discrimination Act provides that a person discriminates against a woman if '(a) on the ground of her sex he treats her less favourably than he treats or would treat a man'. In order to prove less favourable treatment on grounds of sex in a job evaluation scheme, what must be shown is that the woman's job was undervalued because it was performed by a woman rather than a man. Were it possible to bring the case directly under the Sex Discrimination Act, such less favourable treatment – unlike indirect discrimination – would be incapable of being justified. It is likely that the courts will take a similar view under the equal value Regulations: a reason that is based on sex cannot be justifiable 'irrespective of sex'.

Where aspects of the job evaluation scheme have been manipulated with the intention of disadvantaging women provides an example of disparate treatment on grounds of sex. This may be shown where there is evidence that the employer has altered the preliminary results of the evaluation so as to achieve an outcome which will maintain traditional differentials between men's jobs and women's jobs. This, as we have seen, is a common outcome where a policy-capturing approach has been adopted. The issue may also arise where the evaluation is checked by a 'felt fair' method or where preliminary ratings are altered so as to accord with external salary comparisons.

In all these cases, it can be anticipated that the employer will put forward a neutral reason for altering the initial evaluation – to maintain the integrity of the system, to ensure that the company is in line with the external labour market, etc. Whether the employer's true intention was to perpetuate the low pay of women's jobs thus becomes a matter of evidence.

Direct evidence that the scheme has been 'fiddled' to the detriment of women – such as the statement elicited by the LSE study that a company downgraded two women before implementing an evaluation 'because the salary of one of them would have been unacceptably high'[21] – would be particularly useful. But this is unlikely to be available and it has been accepted by the courts that in order to show less favourable treatment on the grounds of sex, it is not necessary for a woman to produce direct evidence of deliberate bias against women. Circumstantial evidence can be used to infer discriminatory intent on the part of the employer.[22]

Inferences of an intention to discriminate in job evaluation schemes can be drawn from evidence of differences in treatment accorded to women's jobs and men's jobs. For example, evidence may be obtained that the employer was under pressure from men not to eliminate the differential between their job and the women's job, but that such pressure was not applied where it was proposed to remove the differential between those men and another group of men.

A clear example of the use of inferential evidence would be where it was shown that the factors usually considered important by the employer were disregarded in evaluating the woman's work.[23] For instance, there would be an inference of discrimination where the job evaluation scheme regarded noise as a component of working conditions but the evaluator did not take into account typewriter and telephone noise in the analysis of secretaries' jobs. Similarly, it could be argued that disparate treatment is suggested by awarding higher points to male jobs for lifting materials which are comparable in weight to those lifted by women in women's jobs.

Where the evaluation of women's work is affected by stereotyped views of women, it will usually be easier to argue a case of indirect discrimination, but in extreme cases there may be sufficient evidence to demonstrate a case of less favourable treatment on grounds of sex. In an American case, *Thompson* v. *Boyle*,[24] the job evaluation was found discriminatory where the evaluator of a bookbinding job awarded no points for training and experience required in sewing because 'the sewing was of the variety most women know how to perform'.

The job analysis, the choice of compensable factors or the factor weightings may emphasise characteristics which have the effect of resulting in higher pay for men's jobs and a lower evaluation for women's jobs. In most instances, this will raise issues of indirect discrimination. But where it can be shown that this was done deliberately to ensure that the women ended up with a lower score than the men, the purported difference in job characteristics is not the real reason for the difference in the evaluation. It is a pretext. The true reason is that some jobs were done by men and some by women and such discrimination falls within the category of disparate treatment.

INDIRECTLY DISCRIMINATORY EVALUATION SCHEMES

The concept of unlawful indirect discrimination, as set out in s.1(1)(b) of the Sex Discrimination Act, means the application of a requirement or condition to members of both sexes which has a disproportionate impact upon one sex and is to their detriment, and which cannot be justified by the employer. Indirect discrimination thus poses two essential questions: is there a 'neutral' requirement or condition which has an adverse impact upon members of one sex? If so, can the employer justify the use of this criterion?

In determining whether a job evaluation scheme is indirectly discriminatory, therefore, the first question is whether aspects of the scheme have a disproportionate impact upon women (or men). This means nothing more than that the particular factors emphasised by the scheme are more characteristic of the jobs mostly held by men than of the jobs mostly held by women (or vice versa) with the result that jobs mostly held by men have higher wage rates than jobs mostly held by women (or vice versa).

Given that most women work in jobs mainly held by women and most men work in jobs mainly held by men, it will be seen that fundamental conceptual problems immediately arise: for no matter how you describe it, the activities carried out in women's jobs are different from those found in predominantly male jobs. Thus West German studies of activity analysis have shown that, in general terms,

> women's jobs show high values in monotonous dynamic muscle work; tactile sensory feedback; checking and transmission of information; and receptive work and work with high demands on attentiveness. They have low values especially in combining and analysing information; the level of decisions to be made; negative physical environmental influences (except noise); night work; and managerial tasks and responsibility for subordinates and for material assets. On the other hand, men have high classifications in heavy dynamic work; combining and analysing information; the level of decisions to be made; stressful

> physical environmental influences; and responsibility for people and material assets. Low values exist for monotonous dynamic work; repetitive work that requires attentiveness; and transmission of information – just those activities that have high classifications in women's jobs.[25]

It follows from the fact that men and women perform very different work that any particular choice of factors or factor weighting will operate to the advantage of one sex and the disadvantage of the other, in the sense that were different factors chosen or the relative importance of the factors adjusted, the results of the evaluation would be different.

This is a matter of logic. If women's jobs emphasise dexterity and men's jobs emphasise strength, the relative scores of men and women will vary according to the relative weight and points allocated to each factor respectively. Of course, the less the factor associated with women is taken into account, the greater the disparate impact will be and, therefore, disparate impact can be reduced by ensuring that the factors chosen reflect important aspects of the work of both men and women. Failure to do this may result in a finding that the scheme is discriminatory, but this does not resolve the logical problem. Nor can it be resolved by using a 'neutral' factor heading such as 'physical activity'. This ensures that both strength and dexterity are given consideration rather than removing the need to give consideration to both factors.

Thus, even where all dimensions of the man's job and the woman's job have been properly accounted for, if the jobs are evaluated as unequal, there must be a reason for this inequality. By definition, it can only be because the person with the lower score scored less on a particular factor – in which case that factor has a disproportionate impact; or because the factors on which one sex scored high were weighted higher – in which case the weighting has a disparate impact. The problem is the logical outcome of job segregation, of the fact that women and men do different work. Where jobs are segregated by sex, any job evaluation system will have a disproportionate impact (though, as a matter of fact, since women's jobs are normally paid less than men's jobs, the system will usually operate to the disadvantage of women).

For this reason, the search for 'job evaluation schemes free of sex bias', as the terms is bandied about by the Equal Opportunities Commission and others in the sense of a job evaluation scheme which does not have a disparate impact upon women, is a chimera. No such animal exists (and, if it did, it would have a disparate impact upon men), which no doubt explains why no one has yet even purported to set out a job evaluation scheme which is 'non-discriminatory'.

The error that is made is to equate a non-discriminatory scheme with a scheme which does not have a disparate impact. In any event, aside from the inherent logical problems, that women score less than men on a given job evaluation does not mean that the job evaluation is discriminatory in any meaningful sense of the word. There is, after all, the possibility that women's jobs may receive lower scores because the women are genuinely employed on work requiring less skill, effort and responsibility – even if this is in part a function of discrimination in job assignments. The suggestion by the Equal Opportunities Commission, in their job evaluation guide, that 'it is important to check the factor scores of the jobs performed predominantly by female employees and if there are a lot of low scores . . . then the set of factors is discriminatory and should be changed'[26] is wrong under any conceivable standard of discrimination law.

Equally disturbing is the suggestion made in a draft of an EOC booklet on *Judging Equal Value*, designed to assist people making representations at an Industrial Tribunal under the new Regulations.[27] This states:

> It will be necessary to ensure . . . that where choices have been made to limit the number of factors used, this has not been made in such a way as to favour factors more frequently found in jobs of one sex rather than the other. If any weighting of factors is done, this must also be done in such a way as to ensure that the overall weighting does not favour factors found more frequently in jobs predominantly done by one sex rather than the other.

Whether this statement will appear in the published version remains to be seen, but there is something very wrong with it. What is it? Aside from the logical impossibility of completely conforming to its diktat, it would merely create a statistical artefact bearing no relation to any plausible aim of job evaluation or compensation policy, let alone the requirements of the law.

By all means, the employer should have to justify why he chose or weighted factors in a way which favoured men's jobs. But to say that he is not permitted to favour factors found more frequently in jobs of one sex is tantamount to saying that he is not permitted to value aspects of the job which he might legitimately regard of value, simply because it happens that they are more associated with men's jobs than women's. He must ignore elements of a job's content which could be justified as an important aspect of that job. Surely, this amounts to rigging the evaluation process to come out with the desired results and is as unacceptable as manipulating the evaluation to ensure that men's jobs score more highly.[28]

The legal standard which is, in fact, adopted under the Regulations where a job evaluation scheme has an adverse impact upon women is that the employer must justify the evaluation. In the next section, we look at how 'justifiable' is likely to be interpreted in general terms, before returning to consider how such a test may be applied to specific instances of indirect discrimination in job evaluation schemes.

The term 'justifiable' in this context derives from its use in the indirect discrimination provisions of the Sex Discrimination and Race Relations Acts. There it has been the subject of extensive judicial consideration. In the first case to deal with the point at appellate level, *Steel* v. *The Post Office*,[29] the EAT set out guidelines for applying the test. These included: that 'the Industrial Tribunal must be satisfied that the case is a genuine one where it can be said that the requirement or condition is necessary'; that 'the Industrial Tribunal should take into account all the circumstances, including the discriminatory effect of the requirement or condition if it is permitted to continue'; that 'it is necessary to weigh the need for the requirement or condition against that effect'; and that 'it is right to distinguish between a requirement or condition which is necessary and one which is merely convenient, and for this purpose it is relevant to consider whether the employer can find some other and non-discriminatory method of achieving his object'. In effect, the *Steel* case adopted a 'business necessity' test similar to that set out by American courts in the line of cases stemming from *Griggs* v. *Duke Power Co.*[30]

Since *Steel*, however, as the EAT aptly put in *Clarke* v. *Eley (IMI) Kynoch Ltd*,[31] 'the decisions of the Court of Appeal and of this Appeal Tribunal disclose a steady decline in the strictness of the requirements which an employer has to satisfy in order to show that a discriminatory condition is "justified"'. Little remains of the *Steel* guidelines. The leading decision now is that of the Court of Appeal in *Ojutiku and Oburoni* v. *Manpower Services Commission*,[32] in which a construction equating 'justifiable' with 'necessary' was expressly rejected as being too high a standard. Lord Justice Stephenson did accept that the guidelines laid down in *Steel* are 'valuable as rejecting justification by convenience and requiring the party applying the discriminatory condition to prove it to be justifiable in all the circumstances on balancing its discriminatory effect against the discriminator's need for it. But that need', he concluded, 'is what is reasonably needed by the party who applies the condition'.[33] Lord Justice Eveleigh in the leading judgment, however, took an even broader view of 'justifiable': 'if I have to give some explanation of my understanding of that word, I would turn to a dictionary definition which says "to adduce adequate grounds for"; and it seems to me that if a person produces reasons for doing something, which would be acceptable to right-thinking people as sound and tolerable reasons for so doing, then he has justified his conduct'. It was Lord Justice Eveleigh's approach which was adopted by the EAT in its most recent consideration of the question.[34] Finally, in *Mandla* v. *Lee*, in the House of Lords, Lord Fraser of Tullybelton expressed the view that whether a requirement is justifiable is a question of fact for the Industrial Tribunal.[35]

Whether a difference or coincidence in values set by a job evaluation scheme is 'justifiable', therefore, is likely to be interpreted as meaning whether the explanation given by the employer for the evaluation or for the particular aspect in question, which has a disproportionate impact upon women, is one which would be 'acceptable to right thinking persons' as a 'sound and tolerable' reason. It is unlikely that any higher standard of proof will be adopted, especially since, unlike the Sex Discrimination and Race Relations Acts, there is no formal burden on the employer under s.2A(3) to show that his reasons are 'justifiable'.

There are other reasons why such a standard may be regarded as appropriate in the context of discriminatory job evaluation. Job evaluation is essentially a method for systematising subjective judgements. There is no 'right answer', in the sense of an objectively correct evaluation,[36] any more than there is such a concept as a 'fair wage'. This has two consequences. One is that it is inherent in the system that no particular way of evaluating jobs is *necessary* for setting wages. The criterion of whether there are any alternative approaches available which are less discriminatory is illogical in the case of job evaluation schemes since the relative weightings, by definition, at any point, can be adjusted in the women's favour.[37] In the case of job evaluation, the question is not whether the weightings can be adjusted, but whether it is reasonable for them to be adjusted.

This leads to the second consequence. Because there is no objective standard of job worth, it is submitted that it is correct on policy grounds for employers to be allowed reasonable latitude in the way in which a particular evaluation is designed or implemented. The ACAS *Guide on Job Evaluation* puts the point well: 'Job evaluation is not an exact science. The aim is to be systematic, but to some extent any assessment of a job's total demand related to another will always be subjective and thus possibly give rise to difference of opinion.'

If the test of 'justifiable' which is to be adopted is that of a reason which would be acceptable as sound and tolerable by right-thinking people, this appears little different in substance from a test of 'reasonableness in the circumstances', the test of unfair dismissal under s.57(3) of the Employment Protection (Consolidation) Act. This is a standard with which Industrial Tribunals are particularly familiar. As the test of reasonableness has been interpreted, there is a band of reasonableness and a decision can only be regarded as unreasonable if it falls outside that band.[38] Such a test of justifiability, although at first sight harsh on an applicant in an equal value case, would have the effect of limiting the intrusion of Industrial Tribunals into job evaluation systems. In addition, it would ensure that the test for whether a job evaluation, in effect, should be set aside on grounds of a suspicion of discrimination and the test for challenging the report of the independent expert (discussed in Chapter 7) would run along roughly parallel lines. It should be noted again than many of the ensuing remarks on when an employer's evaluation may be regarded as discriminatory are also applicable to the test of whether the independent expert wrongly took into account the difference of sex in his evaluation.

When, in practice, is a Tribunal likely to find a job evaluation with an adverse impact upon women outside the band of reasonableness and, therefore, not 'justifiable'? A job evaluation exercise purports to measure systematically the relative importance of different components of the job to the organisation. This means that the factors chosen to be valued and their weighting should accurately reflect the important features of the job. This suggests the most promising line of attack for complainants. For at each step in the job evaluation process, sex stereotyping can result in insufficient credit being given for important aspects of women's jobs.

In a points rating system, the initial steps require the jobs to be analysed and job descriptions prepared. This can lead to different perceptions as to what is important. Inaccuracies can arise through underestimating the difficulties in women's jobs (a problem which can be particularly acute when benchmark jobs are selected which do not represent the work women do). It has been pointed out that clerk-typists have frequently been regarded as mainly engaging in mechanical operations. However, when workers thoroughly familiar with the job evaluate it, mental and interpersonal job requirements may emerge – such as, 'ability to handle a number of tasks at one time', 'ability to proofread by self', 'ability to keep information confidential' and 'getting information from others on their needs'.[39] A particularly common effect of sex stereotypes is that of evaluators disregarding skills learned by women in non-paid work or at home in defining required education and training.[40] In addition, there are negative conditions commonly found in women's jobs which are frequently not considered at all by evaluators. Examples include confinement to small spaces, restricted body movement, use of magnifying equipment and noise from machines such as typewriters and telephones.[41]

Thus, the definition that is adopted for a particular factor can vary greatly and thereby produce different results. 'Skill', for example, can be defined in terms of the amount of on-the-job training required to reach an acceptable standard for the position or it can be defined by the level of full-time education necessary for the post. If men's jobs have formal educational qualifications attached to them and women's jobs do not, but require greater on-the-job training, such a definition will operate to women's disadvantage.

Because, as we have seen, men and women frequently do very different work, the selection of compensable factors and their weighting can result in the relative undervaluation of women's work. Illustrations of how it is alleged that women's work is undervalued are legion. Take the broad heading of 'effort'. Men's jobs frequently receive extra points for the strength required in occasionally lifting heavy weights in comparison with women who may repeatedly lift light weights. Different results might follow if this factor was measured by total weight lifted per work day or according to total caloric output expended.[42] Daniel Leach, former member of the American Equal Employment Opportunity Commission, gives the example of women working on conveyor belts doing assembly work who are evaluated less than men at the end of the belt lifting something that weighs 35 lb every ten minutes and stacking what the women are assembling: 'while the pay difference is sought to be justified by virtue of the fact that supposedly the man is using more energy than the woman, the value is actually reversed . . . We know today that a hand and eye co-ordination job often requires more energy, more effort, more concentration, is more taxing'.[43] Similarly, the physical effort entailed in jobs may be measured by the strength required (which may benefit the evaluation of men's jobs) or by the fatigue induced (which may benefit women). Failure to include manual dexterity in the definition of physical effort will disadvantage women, and emphasis on physical effort in comparison with mental or visual effort (such as in inspection jobs) may assist men.[44]

In assessing 'skill', the complexity involved in simultaneously processing a variety of inputs characteristic of many secretarial jobs may not be given credit.

In assessing 'responsibility', evaluators may tend to give credit for responsibility for property, more characteristic of men's jobs, but downplay responsibility for people, which is part of many women's work.

Whether the stress sometimes associated with women's work is adequately reflected in the evaluation of 'working conditions' is another issue. Women's work is frequently associated with constant interruptions, repetitive tasks, noisy machinery and confined work space.[45] To illustrate just how easy it is to undervalue important dimensions of a woman's job in this connection, we need go no further than the example of discrimination in job evaluation given by the Equal Opportunities Commission in their booklet.[46] This compares the male job of maintenance fitter and the female job of company nurse. As an example of 'unbiased scores', the EOC gives the fitter six points for 'working conditions' and allocates the company nurse only one point. Yet had proper account been taken of, for example, the hazards to the nurse of contracting contagious diseases or the emotional anguish entailed in treating serious workplace accidents, surely such a disparity in scores would not be justified.

This and the other examples set out above suggest that with sufficient thought and preparation it should not be unduly difficult to demonstrate how a given job evaluation has had an adverse impact upon women. At every step in the process of job evaluation, decisions must be taken and, so long as jobs are segregated by sex, it is inevitable that at least some of these judgements will operate to women's disadvantage.

It is by no means normal practice for an employer to choose job evaluation factors that are fully representative of job content. On the contrary, it is not uncommon for significant aspects of the jobs women do to be ignored altogether when women's work is evaluated. If an employer (or, as indicated, the independent expert) has failed to take account of an important aspect of the job the woman does, the complainant should be able to mount an argument that a reasonable employer would have had *some* regard to the dimension of the job in question – that the accuracy required by the job, or the concentration it requires, or the memory it demands, or the dexterity it entails, and so on, should have been taken into account.[47] In practice, this would be a very difficult argument for the employer to overcome. Relative weight is one question; failure to give any weight is another. It is likely, therefore, that Tribunals will find that it is not 'justifiable' to fail to give credit for an important dimension of the woman's job.

Conversely, the evaluation may be attacked where it has given credit for something for which it is not reasonable to give credit. This may be particularly important where the job in question has changed over time, but the evaluation has not been updated – for example, a high score for lifting in the man's job where the work is now done by machinery.

There may also be cases where the employer has clearly erred, such as where he has given importance to factors which are not of genuine significance for the jobs under review – a high rating for experience in the job, for example, where the job can be learned very quickly. Such an anomaly is particularly likely to arise where a proprietary scheme has been bought by the company and the factors used are not meaningful in its own working environment. Factors developed for a job evaluation in a steel mill should not be applied in a bank. Another common error is for the choice of factors to overlap and thus partially duplicate the characteristics of men's jobs. The EOC gives the example of using both 'strength required' and 'sustained physical effort'; a high score on one will normally be associated with a high score on the other.[48]

Suppose the employer has taken some account of the factors associated with women's jobs, but not as much as the woman thinks right. Whether the weight given by the employer to particular factors is justifiable must be largely a question of fact and degree. At the extreme, the weighting will be so manifestly wrong that no reasonable person could think that it accurately reflects the importance of the function to the organisation in question. Extreme weights given to factors which are exclusively found in jobs performed mainly by one sex may be particularly open to attack. A reasonable employer, it may be argued, would not value physical effort as three times as important as mental effort or manual dexterity. But failing that, the relative weighting may be regarded as a matter of opinion on which reasonable men and women could reasonably differ. Once it is accepted that there is no objective standard of job worth, this appears inevitable.

ANNEX I: DISCRIMINATORY JOB EVALUATION SCHEMES AND THE SEX DISCRIMINATION ACT

The 1970 Equal Pay Act provides a right to equal pay where work has been rated as equivalent under a job evaluation scheme but no right to complain that the work would have been rated as equivalent had the evaluation not been discriminatory, except in the limited circumstances where the evaluation discriminates on its face by expressly according 'different values for men and women on the same demand under the same heading'. The new Regulations offer a claimant the opportunity of an independent evaluation where the Tribunal concludes that there are grounds for determining that the employer's evaluation was discriminatory. But if, in the event, the woman's work is held to be unequal to that of her male comparator, what happens to the job evaluation scheme that has been stigmatised as discriminatory? What recourse, for that matter, have other female employees in the organisation whose work has been evaluated under the same discriminatory scheme?

It has long been assumed that existing legislation provided no remedy against discriminatory job evaluation *per se*. But there are no appellate decisions to support this view and the only reported case to even touch on the point was an early

Industrial Tribunal decision.[49] There is no question that neither the Equal Pay Act itself nor the new amendment provide an express remedy for discriminatory job evaluation. But is there scope for bringing a claim under the Sex Discrimination Act? S.6(2)(b) of the Sex Discrimination Act provides that subjecting a woman to a 'detriment' on discriminatory grounds is unlawful and in *Jeremiah* v. *Ministry of Defence*,[50] Lord Brandon in the Court of Appeal construed this expression as meaning 'putting under a disadvantage'. Thus, it could not be seriously contended that a woman whose job has been discriminatorily valued as below that of a man has not been put at a disadvantage.

The reason why discriminatory job evaluation is thought to be outside the scope of existing legislation lies in the overlap provisions of the Equal Pay and Sex Discrimination Acts. S.6(6) of the Sex Discrimination Act provides that: 'Subsection (2) does not apply to benefits consisting of the payment of money when the provision of those benefits is regulated by the woman's contract of employment.' This clearly rules out a claim that a woman should be paid more because her pay was discriminatorily depressed as a result of a job evaluation exercise. There is nothing in s.6(6) excluding the application of s.6(2) in respect of 'detriments'.

Thus it is by no means certain that s.6(6) precludes a challenge to the evaluation process itself rather than to its results – that is to say, the method of arriving at points can be attacked even if the translation of points into pence is immune.[51] The argument is that the process of job evaluation – the drawing up of job descriptions, the job analysis, the choice of compensable factors and even the factor weightings – are not 'benefits consisting of the payment of money'. Nor, for that matter, is there usually anything in an employee's contract of employment regulating how these processes are to be carried out. They may be processes which ultimately result in the payment of money, but so does a selection or promotion procedure! Support for this reasoning derives from no less an authority than the House of Lords. In *O'Brien* v. *Sim-Chem Ltd*,[52] Lord Russell pointed out that the job evaluation study itself and the process of attaching rates to the result of the study were two completely different exercises:

'The fact is that the exercise of equivalent work rating pursuant to a study undertaken under s.1(5) does not determine in any sense any term of the woman's contract.'

It is submitted, therefore, that it is arguable that discrimination in the way a job evaluation is carried out falls within the purview of the Sex Discrimination Act and can be challenged under both definitions in s.1 of that Act.[53]

If this is correct, it would surely be of the utmost importance. Claims could be brought both by an individual under s.6 and by the Equal Opportunities Commission, acting under s.37 of the Act on grounds that a job evaluation scheme which discriminates in intent or effect constitutes operation of a discriminatory practice. The remedy sought would be to require the employer to remove the discriminatory elements in his scheme – to alter his choice of compensable factors, for example, or to change his factor weighting. It might also be possible for those affected to gain compensation on the basis of the loss suffered as a result of the discrimination.

Perhaps most importantly, if this argument is correct, it would provide recourse where women's work has been discriminatorily *undervalued* but where an *equal* value claim cannot be substantiated.

The stakes are so high that it is surely worth testing out this hypothesis by bringing a claim under the Sex Discrimination Act.

NOTES

1. See, for example, K. D. Ewing ('Equal Pay for Work of Equal Value', *Scots Law Times*, 27 May, 1983) who pointed out:

   An ordinary reading of the Directive, together with a consideration of its purpose, suggests that . . . the existence of a job evaluation or classification study is not conclusive proof that the terms of the Directive have been met. The Directive requires that where a job classification study exists, it must be based on the same criteria for both sexes, and must be drawn up so as to exclude discrimination. Manifestly, discrimination will not be excluded where the study is drawn up in a way which embraces and accepts conventional discriminatory practices and assumptions.

   See also A. Lester, *Leading Counsel's opinion*, Equal Opportunities Commission, March 1983.

2. Some 33 per cent of establishments covered by the survey in 1979 commissioned by the EOC had job evaluation schemes and in 25 per cent the scheme applied to all workers. *EOC Research Bulletin No. 5*, 1981.
3. A claim will be barred only where both jobs have been rated by the same evaluation study. Where the applicant seeks to compare herself to a man doing work evaluated by a different study, s.2A(2)(a) will not apply even if the two studies were very similar, since the same study will not have evaluated the two jobs in question.
4. 'Staff job evaluation', *Industrial Relations Review & Report*, No. 310, 20 December 1983.
5. Equal Opportunities Commission, *Job evaluation schemes free of sex bias*.

   The EOC points out that under this type of scheme 'judgements made by the evaluators can have little standard basis other than the traditional value of the job'.
6. Strictly speaking, the key is whether analytic methods have been used, so that an employer should be able to rely on a scheme which combined both analytic and non-analytic methods.
7. [1977] IRLR 71.
8. [1978] ICR 1.
9. [1980] IRLR 73.
10. [1982] IRLR 307.
11. Linda Clarke, 'Proposed Amendments to the Equal Pay Act 1970 – II', *New Law Journal*, 23 December, 1983.
12. *Pace* Richard Townshend-Smith, *Modern Law Review*, vol. 47:2, March 1984.
13. Nor will this issue be resolved at subsequent stages. If the work is held to be unequal, the inference that the scheme is discriminatory remains in limbo. If the work is held to be equal, the employer must direct his defence under s.1(3) at material differences unrelated to the nature of the job itself.
14. M. Rubenstein, 'Discriminatory Job Evaluation Schemes and the Equal Pay (Amendment) Regulations', *New Law Journal*, 18 November, 1983.
15. [1983] IRLR 209.
16. A. Lester and D. Wainwright, *Equal Pay for Work of Equal Value: Law and Practice*, T. M. S. Management Consultants, 1984.
17. 'The New Equal Pay Law', *Industrial Relations Legal Information Bulletin* 249, 24.1.84.
18. An analogous position under the Sex Discrimination Act would allow a woman who failed to get a job which went to a man to claim discrimination and then immediately transfer the burden to the employer to justify his selection criteria. The only way this part of the Regulations makes any conceivable sense is if you completely forget about the broader implications of the Tribunal's finding and direct your mind only to the question of whether the claim should be thrown out at the screening hearing. Then, if you ignore what amounts to a

triple negative in the relevant sections, you come out with a construction something like that the complaint will not be blocked if the Tribunal concludes that there are reasonable grounds for determining that the fact that the woman's work was rated as of less value than that of the man was unjustifiable. This would then broadly parallel the test to be applied at the screening hearing where the jobs in question have not been evaluated. But, the whole point is that the people concerned cannot forget about the broader implications of the Tribunal's finding.

19. 'Staff job evaluation', *Industrial Relations Review & Report* 310, 20 December, 1983.
20. The Trade Union Research Unit (*Women and Job Evaluation: The Implications of the Proposed Amendment to the Equal Pay Act*, Discussion Paper No. 29, March 1983) warns that: 'The use of multiple regression procedures to determine the weights given to factors to make them best fit the ranking of whole jobs reinforces the status quo, because lower weights will be calculated for the factors which predominate in lower grade jobs and the differentials are multipled by the application of this statistical technique.'
21. Ibid, p. 25.
22. See the extract from *Wallace* v. *South Eastern Education and Library Board* cited in Chapter 8.
23. Perhaps the reverse of this principle may also be relevant. Where all the work is done by men, dirty and physically demanding jobs may be the least regarded. Yet such factors are often used to justify higher pay for men when they are compared with women.
24. [DC DC (1979)] 21 FEP Cases 57.
25. C. Helberger, 'Work Analysis as a Means to Achieve Equal Pay for Working Women', in R. S. Ratner (ed.), *Equal Employment Policy For Women: Strategies for Implementation in the United States, Canada, and Western Europe*, Philadelphia, Temple University Press, 1980.
26. EOC, *Job evaluation schemes free of sex bias*, p. 7.
27. I apologise for quoting from a privately circulated booklet prepared only in draft. The final version was not available when this manuscript was completed. I have taken the liberty of quoting from the draft because it illustrates a particular approach to the problem.
28. I am indebted to Jim Matthewman of IRS for discussing some of the above points with me, though the views expressed are my own.
29. [1977] IRLR 288.
30. US Sup Ct (1971) 401 US 424.
31. [1982] IRLR 482.
32. [1982] IRLR 418.
33. No British judge has gone so far as to suggest that the correct balance to be struck is between the employer's business need and the national interest, as expressed through the legislation, in eliminating discrimination. See *Griggs* v. *Duke Power Co* (1971) 401 US 424 US Sup Ct.
34. *Clarke* v. *Eley (IMI) Kynoch Ltd* [1982] IRLR 482.
35. 1983 [IRLR] 209.
36. As the Clegg Commission (Standing Commission on Pay Comparabil-

ity, Report No. 9, *General Report*, Cmnd. 7995, para. 55) put it: 'no amount of examination of jobs can determine whether or not a given factor should or should not affect pay or whether one factor should have more weight than another . . . The answers to these questions are not to be found in the job; they exist subjectively in the minds of those who perform or manage or evaluate the jobs'.

37. It is submitted, therefore, that McCrudden (*The Industrial Law Journal*, December 1983) falls into this trap in pointing out that the Regulations allow each of the elements of a points rating scheme to be challenged and suggesting that 'the crucial question becomes one of "justifiability" in the same way as under the indirect discrimination provisions of the Sex Discrimination and Race Relations Act, e.g. are any alternative approaches available which are less detrimental to women in their effects'.
38. *British Leyland UK Ltd* v. *Swift* [1981] IRLR 91 CA.
39. *Pay Equity: Equal Pay For Work Of Comparable Value*, Joint Hearings before the Subcommittees on Human Resources, Civil Service, Compensation and Employee Benefits of the Committee on Post Office and Civil Service, United States House Of Representatives, 1982, testimony of Lorraine E. Eyde, p. 881.
40. Mary Witt (*EEOC Hearings*, 1980, p. 128) points out that in the US Department of Labor's *Dictionary of Occupational Titles*, the lowest rated jobs for skill complexity included social service posts such as nursery school teacher, home health aid, child care attendant, foster mother and paid homemaker. 'These female-linked jobs bore DOT skill level ratings identical to those published for the positions of rest room attendant, mud mixer helper, parking lot attendant and poultry wasteman.'
41. Helen Remick, 'Strategies for creating sound, bias-free job evaluation plans', *Job Evaluation and EEO: The emerging issues*, Industrial Relations Counsellors, 1978, p. 88.
42. Testimony of Winn Newman, *EEOC Hearings*, 1980, p. 39. Male jobs are characterised as involving full body movement and women's jobs often tend to involve repeated and confined use of only a few muslces and it is arguable that evaluation systems should give value to both kinds of muscle use. Lorraine Eyde, *Pay Equity* Hearings, 1983.
43. Ibid. Testimony of Daniel Leach, p. 321.
44. The Equal Opportunities Commission (*Annual Report*, 1981, p. 91) has noted that it received complaints from women in engineering in respect of high weightings for experience and physical strength and low weightings for mental and visual factors.
46. EOC, *Job evaluation schemes free of sex bias*, p. 7.
47. This is all based on the assumption that the omission of a relevant factor is, for the purposes of the Regulations, tantamount to giving it a value of 'nil', thus constituting a difference between the values set. See McCrudden, *The Industrial Law Journal*, December 1983.
48. EOC, *Job evaluation schemes free of sex bias*, p. 6.
49. *Meeks* v. *National Union of Agricultural & Allied Workers* [1976]

IRLR 198. *Meeks* was a claim under the Sex Discrimination Act concerned with the application of a condition that to receive a higher hourly rate, an employee had to work thirty-five hours a week. It was held that this requirement, although indirectly discriminatory, was excluded from the scope of the Sex Discrimination Act. However, the point raised in this note was not considered and the case turned on the construction of the word 'benefit' in s.6(2)(a), which was held not to include wages. The significance of 'detriment' in s.6(2)(b) was not raised.

50. [1979] IRLR 436.
51. This is a point which I argued at a conference on wage discrimination organised by Industrial Relations (Services) Training Ltd in association with the Equal Opportunities Commission in 1981. At that time it fell on stony ground.
52. [1980] IRLR 373.
53. This would also be within the spirit, and possibly the letter, of European Community law. In the equal pay infringement proceedings case, *Commission of the European Communities* v. *The United Kingdom*, 1982, the European Court of Justice observed that: 'where a job classification system is used for determining pay it is necessary to ensure that it is based on the same criteria for both men and women and so drawn up as to exclude any discrimination on grounds of sex'.

7 The Independent Expert's Report

If the employer has chosen not to put forward a defence at the preliminary stage, or if his defence is unsuccessful, the Tribunal is then obliged to commission a report from an independent expert as to whether the jobs being compared are of equal value.[1]

The particular expert will be chosen from amongst a panel of eleven men and four women appointed by ACAS. The criteria for the initial appointments were set out by the Chairman of ACAS, Mr Pat Lowry, at a conference in November 1983:

> We will expect applicants to have a good working knowledge of the various job evaluation techniques and some recent practical experience of installing and/or operating job evaluation schemes would be preferable. We would expect the expert to have a good general understanding of industrial relations. Obviously, the expert must be able to work independently and impartially, and be able to produce a clear, unambiguous report.'[2]

In the event, ACAS received a great many applications for the posts. Because of the changes made to the proposed Procedural Regulations discussed below, it is understood that the potential ability to defend a report under cross-examination at an Industrial Tribunal was regarded as an important additional criterion for determining who was to be appointed.

Two omissions from the criteria set out by Mr Lowry are worthy of note. There was no requirement that the expert have any detailed knowledge of discrimination law; nor does it appear that a demonstrable understanding and sensitivity to the issues involved in women's disadvantaged status at work was regarded as essential. Some, but not all, of the experts appointed have proven experience of women's issues and the law. Those who do not may find it a severe handicap. The full list of the first appointees is as follows:

Margaret Attwood, Senior Lecturer in Personnel Management, Anglian Regional Management Centre, Chelmsford.
Colin F. Campbell, Lecturer in Personnel Management, Glasgow College of Technology.
James R. Colville, Lecturer in Industrial Relations and Employment Law, Plymouth College of Further Education.
Terence A. Dillon, Staff Tutor, Industrial Relations at University College of North Wales, Bangor.
Ray Edwards, Head of Industrial Relations, The Industrial Society, London.
James A. Iddison, Formerly Principal Industrial Relations Officer, ACAS.
Joan E. Keough, Formerly Senior Industrial Relations Officer, ACAS.
John R. McErlean, Personnel Manager, London Brick Products Ltd, Bedford.
Jeremy McMullen, Regional Officer, General Municipal and Boilermakers Allied Trade Union.
Lorraine Paddison, Tutor in Human Resource Management, British Gas Management Centre, Stratford-on-Avon.
Albert E. Powell, Formerly General Secretary, SOGAT '82.
Sheila G. Rothwell, Director, The Centre for Employment Policy Studies, The Management College, Henley-on-Thames.
Duncan H. Wood, Fellow in Personnel Management, London School of Economics.
Alan Woods, Deputy Personnel Manager, Tootal Textiles Ltd, Manchester.
Peter Yeeles, Group Industrial Relations Manager, United Biscuits (UK) Ltd, Maidenhead.

THE EXPERT'S POWERS

The expert is given certain powers to assist him in the task of determining whether the work being compared is of equal value. He has the right, under Rule 4(1A), to request the Tribunal to 'require any person who the tribunal is satisfied may have information which may be relevant to the question or matter on which the expert is required to report, to furnish, in writing, such information as the tribunal may require' and to 'require any person to produce any documents which are in the possession, custody or power of that person and which the tribunal is satisfied may contain matter relevant to the question on which the expert is required to report'.

A failure to comply with such a requirement is an offence, punishable by a maximum fine of £100. More importantly, the Tribunal can strike out the employer's notice of appearance (or the employee's application). The Rules of Procedure contain provisions permitting a party to appeal against an order to provide information or documents – Rule 4(2)(a).

Interestingly, although the Tribunal can direct that relevant information and documents be made available to the expert, there is nothing in the Rules to enable the expert to have access to the place of work in order to view the jobs in question. It is presumed that employers will co-operate voluntarily, though just how the expert can evaluate the jobs without seeing them in action is a question yet to be answered satisfactorily. Nor is there anything in the Rules which entitles the expert to question the parties orally, though it must be presumed he will ordinarily seek to do so.

THE EXPERT'S DUTIES

The independent expert must work within the broad statutory requirement that the two jobs must be compared 'in terms of the demands made . . . (for instance under such headings as effort, skill and decision)'. This would seem to impose a minimum requirement that the expert must use an analytic method of assessment which takes into account relevant factors of job content, despite the Minister's statement in the

House of Commons that 'the experts will have experience of industrial relations and the evaluation of jobs, though they will not necessarily be expected to use formal job evaluation in considering the value of the two jobs in question'.[3]

In all other respects, the expert is given great discretion by the Rules and Regulations. Nothing is said about the particular techniques the expert is to use and no attempt has been made to ensure uniformity of approach and to avoid inconsistency. ACAS has correctly taken the view that it does not have power to issue guidelines as to the methods to be adopted. Each expert will work autonomously.

Since a given expert will doubtless have his own preferred evaluation technique, this in itself is likely to pose manifold problems. Two examples will suffice: within a given company, comparisons could arise between the same sets of workers in different parts of the country, and two experts could be called upon to report. It is entirely conceivable that, depending upon the evaluation technique adopted, different results could ensue. Or take the case of a firm with different evaluation systems in place for manual and non-manual staff, faced with a comparison between the two groups. Is the expert to evaluate the jobs on the basis of the system used for manual workers, for non-manual staff, or according to his own pet approach which may approximate neither of the systems in use? Whatever approach is adopted may have repercussions throughout the pay structure.

Nor is the expert given any guidance about what may be termed 'the standard of equality' he is supposed to adopt, other than the criterion laid down in s.1(2)(c) that he must compare the work of the woman and the man in terms of the demands made (for instance under such headings as effort, skill and decision). The bare bones of the comparable statutory test for like work in s.1(4) have thrown up a range of questions requiring judicial interpretation – can contractual obligations be taken into account where these are rarely performed? Conversely, can duties frequently performed but not contractual be taken into account? Do differences between night and day work constitute differences to which regard should be paid? Whether work is of equal value will pose both the same and different questions, and it is one of the most extraordinary aspects of the Regulations and Rules that they have been drafted on the assumption that whether two jobs are of equal value is almost entirely a question of fact and impression. As a consequence, as we shall see, the possibility of judicial intervention has been strictly limited. In view of the importance of ensuring that a proper standard for equality is adopted, we have set out in an annex to this chapter some principles which we suggest as suitable to be taken into account in determining whether work is of equal value.

The express constraints under which the expert will operate are set out in Rule 7A(3). In substance, there are only three stipulations: he must 'take account of all such information supplied and all such representations made to him as have a bearing on the question', he must 'take no account of the difference of sex' and he must 'at all times act fairly'.

The expert is given a minimum of forty-two days to produce his report.[4] Rule 7A(3)(b) requires that before drawing up his report, he must produce and send to the parties a written summary of the information supplied to him and the representations made and he must invite the representations of the parties upon the material contained in his written summary. This is important because it provides an opportunity for the parties to correct errors of fact or omission. Having received these representations, the expert is required – Rule 7A(3)(c) – to 'make his report to the tribunal in a document which shall reproduce the summary and contain a brief account of any representations received from the parties upon it, any conclusion he may have reached upon the question and the reasons for that conclusion or, as the case may be, for his failure to reach such a conclusion'.

CHALLENGING THE EXPERT'S REPORT

The ultimate determination of whether work is of equal value is a question for the Industrial Tribunal. Either party can challenge the expert's reasoning or his conclusion. The Industrial Tribunal can reject the expert's report and commission a new report. It can ask the expert for a supplementary report. Or the expert's report can be admitted in evidence. An Industrial Tribunal cannot decide whether work is of equal value until it has admitted the expert's report in evidence. But once it has admitted the report, it can reach a conclusion which either agrees with the expert's finding on the equal value question or which disagrees with the expert's finding. As the Department of Employment has explained, 'the expert's function is to produce a report on the question of equal value but his report is no more than evidence and may be controverted by other evidence in the normal way'.[5]

The grounds upon which, the extent to which and the ways in which the expert's report and conclusion can be challenged and the Industrial Tribunal's powers in such circumstances are easily the most complex part of the Procedural Regulations. As a result, prayers that the Regulations be annulled were made in both Houses of Parliament[6] and, unusually, the drafting of the Regulations were criticised by the Parliamentary Joint Committee on Statutory Instruments. They said: 'In the Committee's view the status afforded to the expert's report is not made clear by the Procedural Regulations, which should have provided further elucidation on this crucial matter.'[7] The difficulties stemmed mainly from the legislative history of the new law, discussed in Chapter 3. When the Procedural Regulations were extensively re-drafted to meet representations, the substantive amendment Regulations had already been approved by the House of Commons so that the language of those Regulations could not be altered.[8] This constraint has produced a statutory framework of regrettable complexity. However, upon analysis, it is suggested that the framework, albeit extremely convoluted, appears to hang together coherently.

To understand the procedure set out in the Rules, it is necessary to distinguish between the broad discretion conferred upon the Industrial Tribunal to determine whether work is of equal value and the more limited rights of the parties to challenge the expert's report. The draftsman has sought to strike a balance between, on the one hand, avoiding a complete re-hearing of the evidence submitted to the independent expert and, on the other hand, permitting sufficient material to be presented to the Industrial Tribunal to enable it to exercise its judicial function of deciding the question posed by the statute.

The procedure begins once the expert has sent his report to the Industrial Tribunal. When the Tribunal has received the expert's report, it must send a copy of the report to the parties and fix a date (at least fourteen days after the date on which the report is sent to the parties) for the hearing of the case to be resumed – Rule 7A(6).

Upon the resumption of the hearing, the Industrial Tribunal must determine whether or not to admit the expert's report in evidence. Although in form this is only a preliminary question, as we shall see the restrictions on evidence once the report has been admitted suggest that, in substance, this is the key opportunity for challenging the report and its conclusions.

Rule 7A(8) lists three broad grounds upon which the Tribunal may decide not to admit the expert's report as evidence, and Rule 7A(9) allows the parties to make representations, give evidence, and call and question witnesses on any matter relevant to those three grounds.

The first ground for challenging the expert's report is that he has not complied with a stipulation set out in Rule 7A(3) – that he has failed to take into account information supplied to him or representations made, that he has not sent a summary of his report to the parties or made his report to the Tribunal in the prescribed manner, that he has not acted fairly, or that he has taken account of the difference of sex.

The expert's report can also be challenged on grounds that its conclusion is perverse – 'that the conclusion contained in the report is one which, taking due account of the information supplied and representations made to the expert, could not reasonably have been reached'.

Finally, the report can be attacked on grounds that 'for some other material reason (other than disagreement with the conclusion that the applicant's work is or is not of equal value or with the reasoning leading to that conclusion) the report is unsatisfactory.[9]

In order to justify any of these contentions, Rule 8(2A) gives either party the right to require the expert to attend the hearing. The expert can be cross-examined on his report and on any other matter pertaining to whether the work in question is of equal value.[10]

Rule 7A(9) gives the Tribunal discretion to permit a party to give evidence upon, call witnesses and question any witness about any matter relevant to Rule 7A(8) – i.e. whether the expert's report is defective. Importantly, Rule 8(2B) gives each party an absolute right to call *one* witness of their own to give expert evidence on whether the two jobs under consideration are of equal value. The 'battle of experts' is likely to be the centrepiece of the Industrial Tribunal hearing. In general terms, given the subjective nature of job evaluation, it should not be difficult for both parties to find 'experts' to support the conclusions for which each is contending.

As a matter of procedure, it should be stressed again that a party seeking to persuade the Tribunal that the expert has erred would be well advised to call all its pertinent evidence *before* the expert's report has been admitted, as part of a challenge to the expert's report. For once the expert's report has been admitted in evidence by the Industrial Tribunal, it is no longer possible to question its factual basis.[11]

How can the expert's report be challenged? Assuming that the expert will normally have complied with the procedural requirements in making his report and will have acted fairly, in practice challenges to the expert's report are likely to be based on one (or more) of three substantive grounds.

The first is that the expert misdirected himself by taking into account something which he should not have taken into account, or by failing to take into account something which he should have taken into account, either of which may be regarded as a 'material' reason for attacking the report. For example, the expert may appear to have failed to take into account a relevant aspect of one of the jobs in reaching his conclusion, perhaps through oversight or because this dimension did not come out when he observed the job. Conversely, the expert may have based his conclusion on activities which were not normal parts of the job in question.

The second ground is that the expert failed to 'take no account of the difference of sex'. In the context, it seems reasonable to interpret this stipulation as meaning that in arriving at his conclusion the expert did not discriminate on grounds of sex within the meaning of the statutory definition. On that basis, where the expert's evaluation has determined that the jobs are of unequal value, the capacity of the expert to stand up to rigorous cross-examination is likely to be sorely tested. All the considerations we discussed in Chapter 6 in the context of discriminatory job evaluation will now be relevant. Whatever factors were used to decide that the jobs were unequal will have to be defended and justified by the expert – and this will be in circumstances where the applicant's own expert should be able to point out that if other 'less discriminatory' factors had been used, the results of the evaluation would have been different. As we have suggested, it is a lot easier to show that a job evaluation was sexually discriminatory than to show that it was not discriminatory. How the Tribunals deal with this issue obviously will be a central point in coming months.

Perversity is the last ground on which the expert's report can be challenged – that the expert's conclusion could not reasonably have been reached on the material before him. This is a heavy burden in that it is implicit that it requires a finding that no reasonable expert on the facts before him could reasonably have arrived at that conclusion. Nonetheless, it is not a burden which appears insurmountable. The inherent subjectivity of job evaluation can work both ways. Because it is largely a matter of opinion, it is difficult to say that no reasonable person would have arrived at a particular conclusion. Conversely, however, it is also easier to mount a formidable argument as to why a reasonable person would have arrived at a different conclusion. In the event, much may depend upon the persuasive powers of the respective parties and the expert and, again, on the approach adopted by the Tribunals.

It is important to bear in mind that whilst perversity is the standard for whether the expert's report should be rejected, it is not the criterion for the Tribunal's determination of whether the work is of equal value. As we now go on to discuss, the Tribunal can admit the expert's report but decide, on the basis of the evidence submitted going to perversity, that on the ordinary weight of evidence the expert's conclusion should not be followed.

This is the part of the Regulations that has engendered the most confusion. After the Industrial Tribunal has heard representations from the parties, including evidence and witnesses, the Rules give the Tribunal the discretion to take one of a number of courses:

1. If the Tribunal has not been persuaded by the evidence that the report is defective, it can admit the report as evidence.
2. The Tribunal may form the view that it requires further information or consideration from the expert. In such circumstances, Rule 7A(10) empowers the Tribunal to require the expert 'to explain any matter contained in his report or, having regard to such matters as may be set out in the requirement, to give further consideration to the question'.[12]
3. The Tribunal can decide, on the basis of the grounds set out in Rule 7A(8), not to admit the report. Suppose, for example, the Tribunal were persuaded that the expert had failed to 'act fairly'. In such a case, the Tribunal would probably decide not to admit the report in evidence. The effect of Rule 7A(8) and Rule 7A(13) is that where a Tribunal has decided not to admit the report, the report is regarded as a nullity and the procedure must begin all over again with the Tribunal commissioning a report from a new expert.

But there is a further option open to the Tribunal. Because s.2A(1)(b) of the amendment Regulations stipulates that a Tribunal cannot determine the equal value question without having received the expert's report, the Tribunal cannot decide not to admit the expert's report and decide the case for itself. If the report is rejected, a new report must be commissioned. However, there is nothing in the Rules to prevent the Tribunal from admitting the expert's report in evidence and, because it has been persuaded by the representations that the expert's conclusion is wrong, determining the question of whether the work is of equal value contrary to the conclusion reached by the expert.

This is because where the Tribunal finds the report defective, there is nothing in Rule 7A(8) which obliges it not to admit the report in evidence. The Rule states that 'the Tribunal may, if it thinks fit, determine not to admit the report'.

If the Tribunal is persuaded that the expert has not acted fairly, the obvious course would be to reject the report and commission a new one. As a matter of logic, however, that would not be the appropriate course to take if the Tribunal accepts an argument that the conclusions of the report are perverse.

If the report concludes that the two jobs under study are not of equal value, but the Tribunal, in accordance with Rule 7A(8)(b), forms the view 'that the conclusion contained in the report is one which, taking due account of the information supplied and representations made to the expert, could not reasonably have been reached', it must have reached the conclusion that the two jobs are of equal value. If no expert could reasonably conclude that the work was not of equal value, there would be little sense in the Tribunal deciding not to admit the report so that a new report would have to be commissioned. Rather, the Tribunal in such circumstances should exercise its discretion and admit the report, but determine the case by reaching a conclusion opposite to that of the expert.[13]

That this is how the Regulations should work was suggested by Lord Gowrie, the Government spokesman in the House of Lords, during the debate on the motion to annul the Regulations. He was asked by Baroness Lockwood, 'If the Tribunal, having heard from the official expert and the experts perhaps of the applicant, favours the evidence of the applicant, could the Tribunal, in those circumstances, make a decision in favour of the applicant but in contradiction to the official expert's report?' He replied: 'My Lords, that would be my understanding, yes. I cannot see why that should not be so as the Tribunal is the final arbiter of the issue.'[14]

Thus, even if the expert's report is admitted in evidence, it is not conclusive as to whether the work is of equal value.[15] It is up to the Tribunal to decide how much reliance to place upon it.[16] Although once the report is admitted, the parties are restricted in the evidence they can bring thereafter to attack the report, the Tribunal is entitled to determine the case on the balance of all the evidence brought before it during the proceedings. Whether the initial determination of the equal value question should have been delegated to an independent expert at all is a matter of opinion. But it is submitted that, on a proper understanding and application of these complicated provisions, there is ample scope for the expert's report to be challenged.

ANNEX II: THE MEANING OF EQUAL VALUE

The Regulations provide no guidance on the criteria to be applied for the purpose of determining whether work is of equal value, other than the definition in s.1(2)(c) that equal value is to be judged 'in terms of the demands made' on the woman 'for instance under such headings as effort, skill and decision' in comparison with the demands made on her male comparator.

Although the Regulations give the independent expert a great deal of discretion in forming a view as to whether the jobs under scrutiny are of equal value, the ultimate determination of this question is for the Industrial Tribunal. As we have seen, the Regulations provide scope for cross-examining the independent expert on the criteria he employed and for proferring alternative evidence challenging the expert's report through the use of an expert witness. Therefore, notwithstanding that the Regulations treat the question of whether work is of equal value as largely one of fact (or opinion), it seems likely that this factual question will be determined against a backcloth of legal principles.

Guidance on the correct approach as to whether two jobs are of equal value can be derived from analogous decisions under the 'like work' provisions of s.1(4) of the Equal Pay Act. Additional assistance comes from judicial decisions and administrative interpretations under the American Equal Pay Act,[17] which embodies a standard of equality using the language of job evaluation – equal work is work 'on jobs the performance of which requires equal skill, effort, and responsibility, and which are performed under similar working conditions'.

From these sources, the following guidelines may be suggested:

- An assessment of whether two jobs are of equal value, in contrast to a like work question, requires the demands of the jobs to be balanced against each other both in respect of a particular factor (different kinds of effort) and as between factors (greater effort in one job, greater responsibility in the other).
- In determining whether work is of equal value, it is the actual job duties and not the job description or contractual obligations which are controlling.
- The personal characteristics of those performing the job are not relevant to whether work is of equal value.
- Differences between the work done by women and the work done by men will not render the work of unequal value so as to justify a pay differential if
  (a) they require an insignificant amount of time, or
  (b) they are carried out only occasionally or,
  (c) all those who receive the pay differential do not undertake the additional duties, or
  (d) all those who undertake the additional duties do not receive the pay differential.
- 'Skill' may be defined as including consideration of such factors as experience, training, education and ability.
  (a) Differences in duties requiring the same skill level cannot render the work unequal in terms of skill required.
  (b) Additional duties with a skill level below that of the primary job does not render work unequal.
  (c) It is the requirements of the job for experience, training and education and ability that is relevant, rather than whether they are possessed by the individuals in question.
  (d) The efficiency of an employee's performance in the job is not in itself an appropriate factor to consider in evaluating skill.
  (e) Possession of a skill not needed to meet requirements

of the job cannot be considered in making a determination regarding equality of skill.

(f) That a job is said to require additional skill will not be relevant unless in practice that skill is exercised.

- 'Effort' is concerned with the measurement of the physical or mental exertion needed for the performance of a job.
  (a) Jobs may require equal effort in their performance even though the effort may be exerted in different ways on the two jobs.
  (b) Comparing different kinds of physical effort may involve balancing the physical strength required occasionally to lift great weights with the fatigue associated with monotonous, repetitive tasks or with tasks requiring dexterity.
  (c) Physical effort required can be balanced against mental effort.
- 'Responsibility' is the degree of accountability required in the performance of the job, with emphasis on the importance of job obligation.
- 'Working conditions' may be regarded as encompassing two subfactors – 'surroundings' and 'hazards'. 'Surroundings' measure the elements, such as toxic chemicals or fumes, regularly encountered by a worker, their intensity and their frequency. 'Hazards' take into account the physical hazards regularly encountered, their frequency, and the severity of injury they can cause.
- Work is not of unequal value because it is carried out at different hours.

NOTES

1. The Tribunal's requirement to the expert must set out the name and address of each of the parties, the address of the establishment at which the applicant is employed, the question to be determined and the identity of the person with reference to whose work the question arises – Rule 7A(2).
2. Rubenstein and Kent Associates Ltd. Mr Lowry added that the experts would receive appreciation training on the legislation; Industrial Tribunal procedures; the role of ACAS in individual conciliation, advisory work and collective conciliation; the role of the expert and the preparation of the report; and the role of the EOC.

3. *Hansard*, House of Commons, 20.7.83, col. 484.
4. If the expert has not produced his report after forty-two days, either of the parties can apply to the Tribunal and, according to Rule 7A(5), if 'the tribunal forms the view that there has been or is likely to be undue delay in receiving that report, the tribunal may require the expert to provide in writing to the tribunal an explanation for the delay or information as to his progress and may, on consideration of any such explanation or information as may be provided and after seeking representations from the parties, revoke, by notice in writing to the expert, the requirement to prepare a report'. In such circumstances, a new expert will be appointed and the process will begin again.
5. *13th Report From the Committee on Statutory Instruments*.
6. *Hansard*, House of Commons, 1.2.84; House of Lords, 1.2.84.
7. *13th Report from the Committee on Statutory Instruments.*
8. That is, without withdrawing the Regulations and laying new Regulations before both Houses.
9. According to the Department of Employment (*13th Report From The Joint Committee on Statutory Instruments*), these three grounds 'have a common thread in that they strike at the essential validity of the report; they are concerned with the question whether the report has been properly prepared. The purpose of the rule is therefore to enable the Tribunal to refuse to accept the report in evidence and commission another if it discovers sufficient impropriety to make the findings of the report unsafe'.
10. The ways in which the report can be challenged by the parties were changed substantially by the Government from the original proposals following widespread criticism that the proposed Rules did not comply with EEC obligations to ensure that the right to equal pay is determined by a fair and effective judicial process to which the claimant has unhindered access. The Consultative Draft of 6 September 1983 provided that the independent expert would not be compellable as a witness and that no evidence or witnesses could be called as to whether the work in question was of equal value. There were also changes to the grounds upon which the report could be attacked, but these were more in form than in substance. Although the only express constraint in the Government's original proposals was that 'the expert shall take due account of any representations made to him by the parties and act fairly', and the report could only be overturned by reason of a failure to comply with that stipulation or on grounds that 'for some other material reason (other than disagreement with the conclusion that the applicant's work is or is not of equal value or with the reasoning leading to that conclusion) the report is unsatisfactory', administrative law principles probably would have permitted a report to be challenged on grounds that the expert failed to take into account facts which he should have taken into account, or took into account facts which he should not have taken into account, or that he misdirected himself in law.
11. Rule 8(2C) stipulates that, 'Except as provided in Rule 7A(9) or by

paragraph (2D) of this Rule, no party to a case involving an equal value claim may give evidence upon, or question any witness upon any matter of fact upon which a conclusion in the report of the expert is based'. As we have seen, however, Rule 7A(9) permits a relatively broad challenge to the expert's report. Rule 8(2D) provides that, notwithstanding the general prohibition in Rule 8(2C), a Tribunal may permit a party to give evidence upon, to call witnesses and to question any witness upon any matters of fact upon which a conclusion in an expert's report is based if either

(a) the matter of fact is relevant to and is raised in connection with whether the employer has shown a defence under s.1(3) of the amended Act, or

(b) the expert's report contains no conclusion on whether the work being compared is of equal value and the Tribunal is satisfied that the absence of that conclusion is wholly or mainly due to the refusal or deliberate omission of a person required to furnish information or to produce documents to comply with that requirement.

This prohibition was heavily criticised during the House of Lords' debate on the motion to annul the Regulations. Lord Gowrie, for the Government, explained that prior to the report being admitted in evidence, the parties would have had two opportunities to draw attention to mistakes or omissions of facts in the expert's report – in making representations on the written summary of the report and in the consideration of whether the report should be admitted under Rule 7A(8). Rule 8(2C), according to Lord Gowrie, 'merely seeks to ensure that such evidence is brought at the appropriate time'. The rule applies only after the expert's report has been admitted by the Tribunal as evidence. 'It would surely be superfluous to re-open questioning on facts at this late stage and would serve only to lengthen tribunal proceedings and to encourage parties to withhold relevant evidence', he claimed. *Hansard*, House of Lords, 1.2.84, col. 742.

The two exceptions provided for by Rule 8(2D) are where the expert has reached no conclusion on the equal value question and the Tribunal is satisfied that the reason for this is wholly or mainly due to the refusal or deliberate omission of a person required by the Tribunal to furnish information or to produce documents and, secondly, where the matter of fact relates to the genuine material factor defence under s.1(3).

12. In that event, the expert must make his reply in writing to the Tribunal and the Tribunal will send a copy of the reply to the parties and permit the parties to make representations upon it. Rule 7A(12) specifies that 'the reply shall be treated as information furnished to the tribunal and be given such weight as the tribunal thinks fit'.

13. Were this not permissible, the language of Rule 7A(8) allowing the Tribunal discretion not to admit the report would be peculiar. If the report was found to have been defective within the meaning of Rule 7A(8), there would be no justification for the Tribunal having any

discretion about not admitting it if the consequence of admitting the report in all cases was that its conclusion could not be overturned.

14. *Hansard*, House of Lords, 1.2.84, col. 744.
15. Richard Townshend-Smith (*The Modern Law Review* vol. 47: 2, 1984) states that, 'If the report is admitted by the Tribunal that conclusively determines the equal value question.' It is submitted that that is incorrect.
16. In answer to the Parliamentary Joint Committee on Statutory Instruments which questioned whether Lord Gowrie had been misleading in telling the House of Lords that 'It is for the Tribunals to decide what weight to attach to all the evidence, and ultimately to decide the issue', the Department of Employment stressed that 'there is no provision in the Rules affording special status to the report once it has been admitted. It is left to the Tribunal to hear and assess all the evidence before it and to decide accordingly. (*13th Report from the Committee on Statutory Instruments*).
17. Equal Pay Act 1963, enacted as s.6(d) of the Fair Labor Standards Act 1938.

8 The Employer's Defence

If the Industrial Tribunal concludes that the work being compared is not of equal value, that is the end of the case and the application will be dismissed. If the Tribunal's conclusion is that the work is of equal value, the employer has the opportunity to put forward a defence under the amended s.1(3) of the Act. Even if the woman's job and the man's job are held to be of equal value, the claim for equal pay will not succeed if the employer can show 'that the variation is genuinely due to a material factor which is not the difference of sex'.

The wording of the amended s.1(3) differs significantly in one respect from the employer's defence to a finding of like work or work rated as equivalent. In the former cases, the material factor explaining the variation must be shown to be 'a material difference between the woman's case and the man's', whereas where work is of equal value, the material factor 'may be such a material difference'. In all other respects, however, the language of the employer's defence is identical. It follows that, for the most part, except where the change in wording is relevant, existing case law interpreting s.1(3) will serve as precedent for the employer's defence to a claim for equal pay for work of equal value. This means that the factor relied on by the employer must be the genuine cause of the variation in pay and not a pretext for reasons connected with the sex of the workers concerned and that even if the reason is genuine, it will not serve as a defence if the factor in question adversely impacts upon women and the employer cannot justify its use.

The other difference in substance derives from the different nature of the claims in question. Because the like work test focuses on 'the things' the woman does and 'the things' the man does, whether it was appropriate to consider a factor such as responsibility under the equal work test rather than as a material difference has never been entirely clear. The delineation under equal value claims poses different problems. As a general rule, a factor related to the demands of the two jobs in question – such as responsibility – should be considered by the independent expert and the Industrial Tribunal for the purpose of determining whether work is of equal value, and having been there considered should not be permitted in the same guise to form part of the employer's defence.

Take the example of differences in service. If a particular level of experience is necessary to do the man's job but not the woman's job, that is a factor which should be thrown into the balance on the man's side in determining whether the work is of equal value. If, despite the greater experience required in the man's job, the two jobs are regarded as of equal value, that the man's job requires greater experience cannot be considered again under s.1(3), but that the man himself has longer service may nonetheless justify a differential. This is because length of service here is not related to the requirements of the job but is a function of a compensation policy designed to minimise turnover. This is relatively straightforward where both jobs are covered by service-related increments, because then if the woman had the same service as the man she would receive equal pay despite the fact that her job did not require any particular level of experience. Where the issue becomes more complicated is if the woman's job does not carry with it service increments because, given the nature of the job, the employer is not concerned with rewarding experience. Here, it is submitted, the man's service cannot justify unequal pay because the employer's need to reward experience in the man's job has already been taken into account in assessing whether the jobs are of equal value.

We look below at how the employer's defence under the new law may work beginning with a consideration of the burden of proof.

S.1(3) lays the burden of justifying the difference in pay upon the employer. This means that if the woman's job is of equal value to that of a man and she is paid less, it is presumed that the variation in pay is due to discrimination – the difference of sex – and it is up to the employer to rebut this presumption by showing, on the balance of probabilities, that it is more probable than not that the variation was genuinely due to a material factor which is not the difference of sex.[1]

Because the burden of proof lies upon the employer, it is up to the employer to advance the necessary evidence before the Tribunal. What will this require in an equal value case? Although there is one important difference in the wording of the equal value defence from the defence in other equal pay cases, in all other respects the language is the same. Therefore, the existing case law on the burden of proof should be applied.

An analysis of the statutory language and the existing case law under the Equal Pact Act suggests that the burden on the employer can be broken down into four elements.[2]

First, the employer has to show the genuine reason for the variation in pay. Secondly, the employer's reason must explain the whole of the variation. Third, that reason must be material, in the sense of it being something which is reasonably required to achieve a legitimate business objective. Lastly, the employer's justification for the differential cannot be tainted by sex discrimination.

GENUINE REASON

The burden is on the employer to show the reason for the variation in pay. He must explain why, in fact, the man was paid more than the woman despite their being employed on work of equal value. The requirement that the variation 'is genuinely due' to a material factor which is not sex-based means that an after-the-fact rationalisation for the differential is not acceptable. In such circumstances, the variation is not 'due' to that factor. Nor can an employer rely upon a reason which, though acceptable on its face, upon investigation is discovered to be a pretext for the true reason, the difference of sex. The use of the word 'genuinely', correctly understood, imports into the employer's defence under s.1(3) the proscription on less favourable treatment on grounds of sex found in s.1(1)(a) of the Sex Discrimination Act. Where the reason advanced by the employer is a pretext, it is not the 'genuine' reason for the difference in pay. We discuss this concept in more detail below in our consideration of a non-discriminatory reason.

EXPLAINING THE VARIATION

Secondly, it is strongly arguable that the employer must show that the factor relied upon for justifying the pay differential explains the whole of the variation in pay. The wording of the statute does not refer to the employer justifying 'a' variation in pay; it requires the employer to justify 'the' variation. The use of the word 'the' must be taken as signifying that the employer must justify all of the variation that exists. That some of the variation in pay can be justified by reason of a material factor should not be regarded as a permissible explanation if the rest of the variation is not due to the material factor, but is due to sex discrimination. This approach was accepted by the EAT in *National Coal Board* v. *Sherwin and Spruce*,[3] where a pay differential for employees on like work was found to be partly due to the fact that the man worked nights and partly due to the difference of sex.

MATERIAL FACTOR

Thirdly, the employer must prove that the factor to which the variation in pay is due is 'material' to explaining a difference in pay. This means that it is not sufficient for the employer simply to show that sex discrimination played no part in the differential. According to the European Court of Justice, the difference in pay must be 'attributable to factors which are objectively justified'.[4] Expanding on that dictum in the seminal case of *Jenkins* v. *Kingsgate (Clothing Productions) Ltd No. 2*,[5] the EAT held that s.1(3) imposes on the employer 'the onus of proving that the variation in pay is *in fact* reasonably required' to achieve a legitimate objective 'which the employer desires for economic or other reasons'.

The distinction drawn by these cases is crucial. If the test of whether a difference is 'material' was purely subjective, it would be sufficient for the employer to argue that he acted in 'good faith' in paying the man more than the woman, that he genuinely thought the man's work was of greater value. Were such a defence conclusive, it would restrict successful claims to those in which it could be shown that sex played a part in the pay differential. But, as Lord Denning put in *Fletcher* v. *Clay Cross (Quarry Services) Ltd*,[6] 'the issue does not depend on the employer's state of mind . . . The employer may not intend to discriminate against the woman by paying her less: but, if the result of his action is that she is discriminated against, then his conduct is unlawful, whether he intended it or not'.

Thus, as the EAT has held, s.1(3) requires consideration of whether the variation is genuinely due to a material difference 'before going on to consider whether that material difference is a difference other than sex'.[7] Although, as we shall see, the courts have verged on permitting a subjective justification in their treatment of red circle defences and defences based on the operation of grading systems, such decisions must now be regarded as of questionable authority in light of the more recent decisions by the European Court and by the EAT in the *Jenkins* case.

The *Jenkins* line holds that the factor relied on by the employer to explain the difference in pay must be objectively justifiable, but when will an employer's reason be so regarded? To answer that requires consideration of the Court of Appeal's decision in the 'market forces' case of *Fletcher* v. *Clay Cross (Quarry Services) Ltd*. The effect of that decision was to restrict a potentially justifiable reason for a differential to one which was based on the 'personal equation' of the employees concerned rather than a reason based on 'extrinsic forces'. Whilst the words of s.1(3) emphasised by the Court of Appeal to support their construction were that the variation must be due to a material difference 'between her case and his', the effect of the decision was to dichotomise between potentially acceptable and unacceptable justifications for the difference in pay. Reasons relating to the 'personal equation' of the employees were potentially permissible: 'the personal equation of the man may warrant a wage differential if he has much longer length of service, or has superior skill or qualifications; or gives bigger output or productivity; or has been placed, owing to down-grading, in a protected pay category, vividly described as "red-circled"; or to other circumstances personal to him in doing his job."[8] Any extrinsic forces which led to the man being paid more could not justify a differential.

On the authority of *Clay Cross*, an employer cannot defend a difference in pay for employees on like work or work rated as equivalent if it is based on circumstances extrinsic to the personal equation of the employees concerned. The Government specifically responded to the Court of Appeal's decision by altering the defence for equal value claims so that the material factor relied on by the employer does not have to be a material difference between the man's case and the woman's case. We consider the effect of this on the market forces' argument separately below. In more general terms, however, until now the binding authority of *Clay Cross* has coloured the approach of the courts to when an employer's justification for a differential was regarded as potentially acceptable.

The real difficulty with *Clay Cross* is that the distinction drawn does not stand up to scrutiny. The dichotomy between personal and extrinsic factors does not provide a workable model. First, the categorisation is not coherent. Market forces, which are categorised as 'extrinsic', can mean nothing more than the rate at which a person is prepared to join a firm or remain in a job. This seems as much a part of his 'personal equation' as his years of service, or that his rate has been red-circled after a job evaluation exercise, or that the rate has been determined by a nationally agreed grading scheme – all defences which have been accepted under s.1(3).

Secondly, on policy grounds, there is no justification for arbitrarily restricting the employer's defence to factors personal to the employees concerned and excluding the employer's business needs. The evil at which both the Equal Pay Act itself and European Community law are aimed is sex discrimination in pay. Provided the employer can show a reason which is objectively justifiable in the sense that it is reasonable to expect that it will achieve a legitimate business purpose, and that reason is neither directly nor indirectly discriminatory, why should the employer be precluded from using such a reason merely because it is extrinsic to the particular workers and outside their personal equation? In any event, it must be assumed that commercial benefit is the normal mainspring of the employer's compensation policy. The dichotomy between differences based on personal factors and differences based on the commercial benefit to the employer is false. Why does an employer reward personal differences if it is not because he perceives it as to his commercial benefit? Long service is not rewarded as a form of cultural approbation; it is an incentive for the employee to stay on so as to reduce the employer's labour turnover costs. Merit differences may be personal to the worker concerned, but they are paid for the employer's benefit.

The extent to which *Clay Cross* remains good law for the purposes of like work or work rated as equivalent claims is not entirely clear. The European Court, in *Jenkins* v. *Kingsgate*, gave as an example of a case where a pay differential may be justified 'where an employer is endeavouring on economic grounds which may be objectively justified to encourage full-time work irrespective of the sex of the worker'. When the case came back to the EAT, it used that passage of the ECJ's rather opaque decision to reject an argument on behalf of Mrs Jenkins that an objective related to the employer's profitability was an extrinsic factor which, on the authority of *Clay Cross*, could not be relied upon. At the least, this limits the application of the *Clay Cross* principle.[9]

More importantly, for our purposes, the new wording of s.1(3) permits the employer to defend an equal value claim on the grounds that the variation is genuinely due to 'a material factor which is not the difference of sex'. That material factor may be, but does not have to be, a material difference between the man's case and the woman's case. The distinction drawn by *Clay Cross*, therefore, will not govern the employer's defence under the new Regulations.

Instead, on the authority of *Jenkins No. 2*, the test that would be applied is whether the reason given by the employer for the difference in pay can be regarded as one which is 'in fact reasonably required' to achieve a legitimate business objective. This suggests that the employer must show that (a) the factor explaining the pay differential was intended to achieve some stated business purpose[10] and (b) that the pay differential actually achieved that objective.

Strictly construed, this poses a very difficult evidential standard for the employer to satisfy. It requires the employer, in effect, to validate the use of the differential. Can an employer show that service increments, for example, actually have the effect of reducing labour turnover among long-term employees? Is there objective evidence as to the benefits received from paying more to honours graduates than to those with ordinary degrees for work of equal value? Whether the Tribunals will apply *Jenkins No. 2* in its full rigour to require such a showing to be made must be regarded as doubtful. There is little to go by from cases under the 1970 Act since it is one of the paradoxes of equal pay law that just at a time when the balance of the case law tilted in the applicant's favour, the number of applications dried up.

NON-DISCRIMINATORY REASON

To fall within the defence provided by s.1(3), the variation in pay cannot be due to 'the difference of sex'. The Court of Appeal in *E. Coomes (Holdings) Ltd* v. *Shields,*[11] held that the Sex Discrimination Act and the Equal Pay Act 'provide in effect a single comprehensive code . . . both Acts should be construed and applied as a harmonious whole'. On that footing, the EAT, in *Jenkins No. 2*, felt entitled to construe the meaning of a 'difference of sex' in s.1(3) by reference to the definition of discrimination in s.1(1) of the Sex Discrimination Act so as to cover both less favourable treatment on grounds of sex and unjustifiable indirect discrimination.

The EAT's vital holding that s.1(3) of the Equal Pay Act forbids unjustifiable indirect discrimination seems the correct interpretation of the statute.[12] It was so regarded by the Government in drafting the new Regulations.[13] However, two important problems of interpretation were raised by *Jenkins No. 2* which remain to be resolved. One is the standard of proof required to justify an indirectly discriminatory material factor mentioned above and discussed in detail subsequently in this section. The other problem derives from the distinction drawn by the EAT between the statutory definitions of discrimination in the Sex Discrimination Act.

In explicating the distinctions between the statutory definitions of discrimination, the EAT fell into the trap of limiting so-called 'direct discrimination' to cases of overt discrimination on grounds of sex and dividing cases of indirect discrimination into cases which are 'intentional or unintentional'.

> We use the phrase 'direct discrimination' to mean cases where a distinction is drawn between the rights of men and the rights of women overtly on the grounds of their sex. 'Indirect discrimination' covers cases where, because a class of persons consists wholly or mainly of women, a difference drawn between that class and other persons operates in fact in a manner which is discriminatory against women, e.g. the present case. Indirect discrimination may itself be either intentional or unintentional. It is intentional if the employer (although not overtly discriminating) treats the class differently because he intends to differentiate on grounds of sex, i.e. he is dissimulating his real intentions. Indirect discrimination is unintentional where the employer has no intention of discriminating against women on the grounds of sex but intends to achieve some different purpose, such as the greater utilisation of his machinery.

Although it follows a distinction drawn by the draftsman under s.68(3) in relation to compensation, it is submitted that the concept of intentional indirect discrimination as set out by the EAT is a contradiction in terms. If the employer 'treats the class differently because he intends to differentiate on grounds of sex', that is not indirect discrimination. On the contrary, it is less favourable treatment on grounds of sex, precisely the mischief at which the proscription on 'direct discrimination' is aimed. In terms of s.1(3) of the Equal Pay Act, if an employer dissimulates his real intentions because he intends to differentiate on grounds of sex, the variation in pay is due to the difference of sex and not 'genuinely due' to the factor relied upon. The distinction is crucial because once it is accepted that the material factor relied upon by the employer is not genuine for the purposes of s.1(3), there should be no requirement on the complainant to show that the spurious factor had an adverse impact upon women nor an opportunity permitted the employer to justify a pretextual reason – standards which would be applied in a genuine case of indirect discrimination.[14]

It is submitted that the correct approach to the definitions of discrimination both for the purposes of the Sex Discrimination Act and s.1(3) of the Equal Pay Act is to distinguish between intentional and unintentional discrimination on grounds of sex. Indirect discrimination does not require a showing of discriminatory intent. If the Tribunal finds that a woman is employed on work of equal value to that of a man, it is up to the employer to advance a justification for the unequal pay. By definition, that reason cannot be because the woman is a woman and it follows that the one certainty is that the employer is not going to stand up and say that the reason for the differential is because the complainant is a woman. The employer, in practice, will always put forward a reason that is neutral in terms of sex on its face.[15] The employer's reason – the material factor purportedly explaining the variation in pay – can then be tested under both theories of discrimination to determine whether it is the true reason *and*, if it is the true reason, whether it was indirectly discriminatory. Thus the same set of facts may give rise to a claim under both theories of discrimination.[16]

An example may be helpful to illustrate this central point in the correct approach to discrimination law. A female secretary has claimed equal pay for work of equal value with a male messenger. The two jobs are held to be of equal value. The employer defends the pay differential on the ground that the man has two 'A' levels and the woman has no 'A' level qualifications. Therefore, the employer says, the reason the man is paid higher has nothing to do with sex.

This reason – the difference in 'A' level qualifications – is gender-neutral on its face. But it can be tested under both definitions of discrimination. First, the woman can attempt to show that the 'A' levels are not the *real* reason why the man was paid more; that it is an after-the-fact rationalisation for the difference in pay and that the true reason for the difference in pay was the difference in sex.

Less favourable treatment on grounds of sex implies that the discrimination is intentional; but to show less favourable treatment on the grounds of sex, it is not necessary for the woman to produce direct evidence of deliberate bias against women. The courts have long recognised that requiring proof of the employer's discriminatory state of mind would place too heavy a burden on the claimant. As an American court many years ago pointed out, an employer 'intent on violating the law against discrimination cannot be expected to declare or announce his purpose. Far more likely is it that he will pursue his discriminatory practices in ways that are devious'.[17] For this reason, the courts have accepted circumstantial evidence to be used to infer discriminatory intent on the part of the employer. The reasoning was clearly set out by the Lord Chief Justice of Northern Ireland (Lord Lowry) in *Wallace* v. *South Eastern Education and Library Board*:[18] 'Only rarely would direct evidence be available of discrimination on the ground of sex; one is more often left to infer discrimination from the circumstances. If this could not be done, the object of the legislation would be largely defeated, so long as the authority alleged to be guilty of discrimination made no expressly discriminatory statements and did not attempt to justify its actions by evidence.'

Returning to our example, if there were other male messengers who did not have 'A' levels but were paid the same as the male messenger with 'A' levels, that would suggest the inference that the 'A' levels were not the real reason for the pay difference between the messengers and the secretary. If, therefore, the employer's stated reason for the variation in pay is shown not to be genuine, but rather a pretext for the woman's sex, then the true grounds for the difference in pay is the difference of sex and the employer's defence cannot succeed.

The disparate treatment theory of discrimination embodied in the definition of discrimination in s.1(1)(a) of the Sex Discrimination Act also applies to cases where the factor the employer claims explains the pay differential has been applied to one sex only. If both men and women have 'A' levels but only the men get higher pay for 'A' level qualifications, the women are treated less favourably on grounds of their sex. This is a fairly obvious concept, but it is likely to prove of importance in equal value claims, particularly where the employer's defence for unequal pay is supposedly based on 'market forces'.

If the factor advanced by the employer to explain the pay differential between the woman and the man employed on work of equal value is genuinely sex-neutral, it can still be challenged on the grounds that it is indirectly discriminatory. This requires the woman to show that the factor relied on by the employer – the 'requirement or condition', has a disproportionate impact upon women in the sense that considerably fewer women than men can comply with it. Using our example, the woman may be able to show that fewer women than men have 'A' level qualifications so that basing pay on possession of 'A' levels has an adverse impact upon women.

If disproportionate impact is shown, the evidential burden of proof transfers to the employer to justify the use of such a criterion. It will be recalled that the European Court, in *Jenkins* v. *Kingsgate*, stated that the difference in pay must be 'attributable to factors which are objectively justified' and that, in *Jenkins No. 2*, the EAT took the view that this required the employer to prove that the variation is in fact 'reasonably necessary in order to obtain some result (other than cheap female labour) which the employer desires for economic or other reasons'. However, as we saw in our discussion of discriminatory job evaluation, subsequent to the *Jenkins* decision the Court of Appeal has considered the meaning of 'justifiable' for the purposes of s.1(1)(b) of the Race Relations Act[19] and all three judges were agreed that 'justifiable' applies a lower standard than 'necessary'. Lord Justice Eveleigh felt that 'if a person produces reasons for doing something, which would be acceptable to right-thinking people as sound and tolerable reasons for so doing, then he has justified his conduct'. The wording of s.1(1)(b) of the Race Relations Act and s.1(1)(b) of the Sex Discrimination Act is identical in material part and in *Clarke* v. *Eley (IMI Kynoch) Ltd*,[20] the EAT adopted Lord Justice Eveleigh's approach in construing s.1(1)(b) of the Sex Discrimination Act. Since the explicit justification for implying the concept of indirect discrimination into s.1(3) of the Equal Pay Act was that that Act should be construed harmoniously with the Sex Discrimination Act,[21] it is certainly arguable that it follows that the criteria for when an employer can justify a variation in pay under s.1(3) set out in *Jenkins No. 2* must be modified to accord with the less strict view of the Court of Appeal.

Where the quasi-reasonableness test adumbrated by Lord Justice Eveleigh seems irreconcilable with the tests set out in *Jenkins No. 2* is in the latter's insistence on the employer showing by evidence that the variation in pay is *in fact* reasonably required to achieve his business objective. A less stringent evidential test, that still ought to meet the standard of objective justifiability laid down by the European Court, is that the employer must show that it was reasonable to expect that the variation in pay would achieve his business objective. Such a criterion would still require the employer to demonstrate a reasonable nexus between the difference in pay and his business objective, but it would relieve the employer of the additional burden of producing evidence – which in many cases might be difficult to come by – that his business objective was actually achieved by the variation in pay.[22]

As with so much else under the new Regulations, all that is certain now is that this issue provides ample scope for litigation. With this thought in mind, we turn now to consider some of the main reasons which will be advanced by employers to justify unequal pay for work of equal value. We begin with the controversial question of market forces.

MARKET FORCES

Can an employer pay a man more than a woman performing work of equal value because of shortages of staff, or labour turnover, or the existing market rate, or in order to attract him from another job or to ensure that he does not leave? The extent to which these factors, which fall under the general rubric of 'market forces', will be permitted as a defence to equal value claims is probably the single most important issue which will be determined by the courts and tribunals under the new Regulations.

A 'market forces' defence was rejected by the Court of Appeal as a justification for higher payment of a man employed on like work in the case of *Fletcher* v. *Clay Cross (Quarry Services) Ltd*, where the employer contended that he had to pay the man more than Mrs Fletcher because he was earning more in his previous employment and would not join the company for a lower rate. The Court of Appeal held that the language of s.1(3), requiring the employer to prove that any variation between the pay of a woman and that of a man employed on like work was genuinely due to a material difference (other than sex) 'between her case and his', meant that there must be a difference in the 'personal equation' of the woman as compared with the man. Giving the leading judgment, Lord Denning said: 'An employer cannot avoid his obligations under the Act by saying: "I paid him more because he asked for more", or "I paid her less because she was willing to come for less". If any such excuse were permitted, the Act would be a dead letter. Those are the very reasons why there was unequal pay before the Statute. They are the very circumstances in which the Statute was intended to operate.' It was because the Court of Appeal stated in terms that market forces were not a difference 'between the man's case and the woman's case' that the Government introduced different wording with respect to the defence of equal value claims than applies to like work or work rated as equivalent claims. The amended s.1(3) states:

> (3) An equality clause shall not operate in relation to a variation between the woman's contract and the man's contract if the employer proves that the variation is genuinely due to a material factor which is not the difference of sex and that factor
>
> (a) in the case of an equality clause falling within subsection (2)(a) or (b) above, must be a material difference between the woman's case and the man's; and
>
> (b) in the case of an equality clause falling within

> subsection (2)(c) above, may be such a material difference.

In introducing the Regulations in the House of Commons, the Minister (Mr Alan Clark) explained the Government's intention as follows: 'The draft regulations specifically provide that in these equal value cases the defence of material factors may go wider than the current defence of material difference other than the difference of sex. What we have in mind are circumstances where the difference in pay is not due to personal factors between the man and the woman, but rather to skill shortages or other market forces. If a man is paid more than a woman for work of equal value because his skills are in short supply, this is not sexually discriminatory, provided the reason is genuine and the employer can show this.'[23] And in the House of Lords, Lord Gowrie gave some examples:

> Let us suppose that a female clerk claims equal pay with a male computer programmer on the grounds that her work is of equal value to his. The employer might admit that the work is of equal value but might argue that he has to pay the computer programmers more in order to retain their services, otherwise they would simply leave for higher pay elsewhere. This is a perfectly valid reason for a difference in pay because it is not based on sex. Another example: local education authorities who need to attract mathematics teachers in shortage areas can offer them a lead in pay over other teachers starting their careers. This is to do simply with the shortage of maths teachers; it has nothing whatsoever to do with sex discrimination – and, of course, it applies to either sex.[24]

To the extent that market forces are based on the fact that women will work for a lower wage than men, it would annihilate the concept of equal pay for work of equal value were such a defence to be regarded by the courts as conclusive. A market forces' defence, if always permitted, would undercut the EEC Equal Pay Directive and the

European Court's decision and would be unlikely to comply with European Community law. The main reason why women are paid less than men for work of equal value is precisely because the employer can attract and retain them for a lower wage. As we saw in Chapter 2, because of discrimination, the labour market does not operate in the same way for women and men. The underlying premise of all equal pay legislation is that the labour market is contaminated by sex discrimination and the whole point of such legislation is to interfere with the operation of the market, even if the price of greater equity may be less efficiency.[25] As an American court bluntly put it, equal pay legislation 'recognises that women, imbued with their traditional subservient place in the social hierarchy, are willing to sell their services more cheaply than men, and it takes steps to prevent employers from taking advantage of that willingness'.[26] The market, therefore, cannot be regarded as an impersonal, neutral abstraction.[27] It is the sum of the behaviour of individual employers and employees. It cannot be right to construe the law so as to allow an employer to pay women less merely because it reflects the market place.[28]

Women's willingness to work for lower wages, however, is not the only example of market forces affecting the wage-setting process. Skill shortages or excessive labour turnover, the two examples given by Lord Gowrie, illustrate other ways in which the labour market commonly affects relative pay. It is very easy to dismiss any defence to unequal pay based on market forces out of hand. Yet there are cogent arguments for permitting market forces to be used, at least in some circumstances, as a justification for paying unequal rates for work of equal value. The market rate, even in a job evaluated structure, is virtually a universal criterion in pay determination. Indeed, far from being regarded as anomalous, reference to the prevailing market rate for different jobs may be considered an essential component of fairness – as in the public sector use of comparability with the private sector. Were employers not permitted to pay more to attract scarce labour, it would produce gross inefficiencies in the labour market. Clearly, wage differences play some function in the allocation of labour and there is no reason for supposing that the EEC Equal Pay Directive or the judgment of the European Court requires the repeal of the laws of supply and demand.[29]

There are also compelling conceptual distinctions between prohibiting a market forces justification for unequal pay for like work and proscribing a market rate defence where work is of equal value. By definition, in a like work case, the man and the woman are performing the same job and are assumed to be interchangeable. If women are available to perform the same job, it is difficult to justify paying men a higher wage because of shortages in the male labour supply. In the case of work of equal value, however, the jobs being compared may have completely different labour supply characteristics.

Most importantly, there are the practical consequences which would ensue if market forces were never permitted as a defence to unequal pay for work of equal value. In any pay structure, there are groups who are paid above their evaluated worth because of labour shortages. Computer programmers are a well-known example. If market forces are never permitted to justify unequal pay for work of equal value, all and sundry will compare themselves with such groups. Once members of one sex established equal pay for work of equal value, there would be knock-on claims for equal pay for like work from members of the opposite sex. The result would be chaos and/or widespread evasion of the Regulations.

For these reasons, it is understandable that the Government used different wording for the defence to equal value claims and it is highly improbable that the courts will rule that market forces are never permissible as a justification for unequal pay for work of equal value.

Always to permit market forces as a defence to unequal pay for work of equal value, therefore, is unacceptable. It is equally unacceptable never to permit market forces as a defence.

What then is the correct standard? When are the courts likely to permit market forces to be used as a defence? The objective of the Regulations is to combat wage discrimination against women. The argument against the use of market forces as a defence rests on the premise that market forces frequently discriminate against women. Therein, it is suggested, lies the key. Does the use of market forces in the particular circumstances of the case discriminate against women either in intent or in effect? Whether an employer who claims that he pays a man more because he needs to do so in order to attract or retain him has a valid defence should be determined according to whether that practice discriminates on grounds of sex either directly or indirectly.

This means that to determine whether market forces are an acceptable defence we must determine whether their use falls foul of the two definitions of discrimination in the Sex Discrimination Act and treated as incorporated into the Equal Pay Act by the EAT in *Jenkins* v. *Kingsgate No. 2*. Market forces cannot justify unequal pay for work of equal value unless they are used in a sex-neutral way. Women must be treated in the same way as men. Even if women are treated in the same way as men, if the use of market forces has an adverse impact on women, the employer must justify their use. In practice, what this means is that the validity of the market forces argument must be determined according to the evidence in each case and tested under both theories of discrimination.

Examining the argument that the men are paid more because of market dictates under the disparate treatment principle, the main issue is whether the use of market forces is a pretext for paying the women less because they are women. This might be inferred where the employer refers to the market rate only in the case of men's jobs and does not consider what the market rate is when setting the pay for women's jobs.[30] The employer must show by evidence that higher rates are necessary to attract or retain labour for one job and not the other – i.e. that both jobs are paid at their market rate. Thus one evidential issue for the employer, who is attempting to defend higher pay for men's grades because of unfilled vacancies, is whether the pay for women's grades is increased when there are shortages of labour in those positions. Does the employer even-handedly respond to scarcities in female-dominated and male-dominated fields? Similarly, it may be argued that an employer who pays 10 per cent above the market rate for all jobs except those mainly occupied by women is treating women less favourably on grounds of sex. On the other hand, if the employer can point to a third group – not mainly composed of women – employed on work of equal value with the complainant and receiving the same wage as her – that will be powerful evidence supporting the argument that the extra payment for the men was genuinely due to market factors.

That the employer uses market forces in a neutral way to determine pay for both men and women is not likely to be a sufficient defence under s.1(3). Since the market rate for 'women's jobs' is lower than for 'men's work', reliance on the prevailing market rate is a 'neutral' policy which, because of historical discrimination, has a disadvantageous impact on women. Under the principles of indirect discrimination, the burden will be on the employer to show that the use of market forces is justifiable. Whatever standard of justification is adopted by the courts, it seems safe to say that a conclusory assertion by the employer that he needs to pay a man more will not suffice. Hard evidence rather than subjective perceptions should be required to discharge the burden of proof.[31] It may be suggested that evidence will be necessary to show, first, the level of the market rate, i.e. that the employer surveyed the market rate for jobs of similar skill, experience and service.[32] Secondly, the employer is likely to have to show that he needed to pay that market rate in order to attract or retain labour. This would require specific evidence of labour turnover for the job in question, or of shortages of workers with certain qualifications, or of difficulties in recruiting workers for the job. Thirdly, for the defence to be valid, those conditions cannot have applied equally to the woman's job.

There is a crucial distinction between paying a group of workers more than their assessed value because of labour shortages and paying a group of workers less than their assessed value because of labour surpluses. The former may be regarded as permissible, provided it is justified by the evidence. The latter amounts to exploitation and is precisely the evil at which discrimination legislation is directed. Thus, none of these defences should be open to an employer who paid men's jobs more because everyone else pays men's jobs more or to an employer who pays women's jobs less because he can get them to work for less. It is implicit in those circumstances that pay for the job is related to the sex of the worker performing it. Far from being a factor other than the difference of sex, sex is the very factor responsible for the difference.

If this analysis is correct, there is one practical consequence of overriding importance: sex cannot be the reason for a pay differential if the workers getting the lower rate are composed relatively equally of men and women. Take the case of two groups of workers, both integrated by sex approximately equally. A woman in group *A* claims that she is employed on work of equal value with a man in group *B*. The employer argues that the man in group *B* is paid more because of the market. The use of the market rate cannot be discriminatory in such circumstances because the men in group *A* get the same lower rate as the women in group *A* (and the women in group *B* would get the same higher rate as the men in group *B*). The key consideration is likely to whether the *complainant's* group is integrated or segregated by sex. That the higher-paid group contains a good proportion of women is unlikely in and of itself to be an acceptable defence, on the reasoning that simply because an employer does not discriminate against some women does not mean that he does not discriminate against other women. There is no hard and fast rule as to what constitutes an integrated occupation, but the US Department of Labor regards an occupation as segregated by sex where one sex comprises more than 70 per cent and this is as good a rule of thumb to follow as any. The best way, therefore, of minimising the potential impact of the new Regulations is to ensure that job categories are integrated by sex.

Given the contamination of the labour market by discrimination, the extent to which adherence to the market rate is permitted to justify unequal pay for work of equal value will be a crucial determinant of the Regulations' effectiveness. That women can be induced to work for lower pay than men on jobs of equivalent value cannot be accepted as a valid justification except by making a mockery of the law. Yet to prevent an employer from responding to genuine problems of recruitment and retention of qualified staff through the use of wage differentials would constitute an unwarranted interference with the efficient operation of business. The task for the tribunals and courts in the coming months will be to strike the correct balance between these two extremes.

Market forces are one possible justification for unequal pay for work of equal value. Case law under the Equal Pay Act suggests a number of other factors which an employer may advance as a defence for unequal pay. The remainder of this chapter looks at other defences and considers their likely effectiveness.

BARGAINING POWER

The possibility has been raised by some commentators on the Regulations that the amended defence may permit employers to argue that the variation in wage rates reflects 'the presence of differential bargaining groups, grades or departments, and is due to the relative collective bargaining strengths of those particular sections of the workforce'.[33]

Whether differences in bargaining power justify unequal pay raises some of the same issues as other market forces arguments, but there are also some special considerations. First, it is submitted that no discrimination issues arise if the group making the equal value claim is composed relatively equally of men and women. Whether it is right or wrong for an employer to accede to bargaining power is not the issue posed by the Regulations. That only becomes relevant where the employer's action is sexually discriminatory in intent or in effect.

If the claimant group is largely composed of women, the question to be answered is why does the employer have to pay more to the men? The simple answer 'collective bargaining strength' does not tell us enough. Taking a hypothetical example of unorganised female clerical supervisors and unionised male chargehands,[34] three possible explanations can be imagined for why the employer would pay the men more. One is that the chargehands would not work at the clerical supervisors' rate. This is not a relevant defence because the issue for determination is whether the clerical supervisors should be raised to the chargehands' rate rather than whether the chargehands' rate should be lowered to that of the clerical supervisors.

A second and related explanation for the clerical supervisors' lower pay may be that the employer can get them to work for less than the chargehands. If such is the case, bargaining power is a pretext for the real reason for the variation in pay and the real reason is one which, as we have seen, is unacceptable.

This leaves us with bargaining power as the genuine reason – that the chargehands insist on maintaining a differential with the clerical supervisors and will use their industrial muscle to enforce it. This reason itself, however, poses a further question: would the chargehands insist on a differential between themselves and the clerical supervisors if the clerical supervisors were not women? If not (and this is a matter of evidence), then the reason why the bargaining power is being exerted is because of sex and such an excuse is clearly impermissible since it is tainted by sex discrimination.[35]

It is only if there is evidence that the men have insisted on maintaining their differential with all lower-paid groups, regardless of their sex composition, that a genuine issue of indirect discrimination may arise on the basis that the employer's acquiescence to the men's bargaining power has a disparate impact on the women if it is their work which has been found to be of equal value. But even here it is unlikely that such a defence would have much prospect of success. Inequality of bargaining power is not a new issue for equal pay law (or for discrimination law generally). The same problem arose in implementing the 1970 Act where men were not happy with the removal of their customary differentials. Inequality of bargaining power – whether in the labour market generally or within an internal labour market – is precisely what equal pay legislation is designed to help rectify, and it is one of the most fundamental principles of discrimination law that an employer cannot excuse his discriminatory acts by blaming his conduct on the demands of others – whether they be his customers or his employees or the trade union with which he deals.

RED CIRCLE RATES

'Red-circling' is the personnel term used to describe a situation where an employee is maintained on a personal rate in circumstances in which the 'rate for the job' would normally be lower. Whether a man employed on work of equal value with a woman is entitled to higher pay on grounds that his rate has been red-circled has led to extensive litigation under the parallel provisions of the Equal Pay Act.

At law, the issue in a red circle case is not whether the man should retain his personal rate (though the courts have frequently lost sight of this). It is whether the woman employed on work of equal value (or equal work) should receive that rate as well. In order to answer that question, it is suggested that a key consideration is why was the man paid more than the woman before the red circle was drawn? In the leading case in this area, the consolidated decisions in *Snoxell and Davies* v. *Vauxhall Motors Ltd* and *Charles Early & Marriott (Witney) Ltd* v. *Smith*,[36] the EAT set out the general rule that an employer seeking to justify a differential on grounds of a red circle cannot establish a defence under s.1(3) when it can be seen that past discrimination has contributed to the variation in pay between the woman and the man. Pointing out that 'there is no such thing as a "red circle answer" to a claim', the EAT stressed that: 'It is necessary to examine the origins of the red-circling, to see whether in other respects the arrangements are unisex and non-discriminatory'. Thus, in the *Vauxhall* case, although the immediate cause of the variation in pay was that the women were not in the red circle, the reason why they were not within the red circle was because women were excluded when the red circle was formed following regrading. Had the women not been women, they would have been within the red circle.

That the man was previously paid more so that it is necessary to protect his rate cannot be the material factor relied on by the employer. What the employer must prove under s.1(3) is not just why it was necessary to protect the man's rate, but that there was a material and non sexually-based reason justifying the man's higher pay.

Red-circling mainly occurs in three kinds of situations.

First, where the employee is no longer capable of performing his previous work, as a result of illness or deteriorating ability, and is moved to a new post which, in the absence of his rate being personally protected, would be lower paid. A second situation is where the relative value of the employee's job has changed, either because the old job has been abolished and the employee has been given alternative employment with a protected rate or because the employee remains in the same post but the job has altered over time, such as through de-skilling or the removal of responsibilities. A third situation in which red circles have been used is where a job has been graded or evaluated and is seen to be attracting a rate that is out of line with comparable work. In such circumstances, existing job holders may nonetheless have their rates protected.

Where the man was employed on work of greater value to that of the woman prior to the red circle being formed, that will assist the employer in discharging the burden of proof, since the reasons why the man's previous work attracted a higher rate will serve as reasons justifying his rate being red-circled. If, through illness, a man is transferred from a job of greater value to a job of equal value with that of the complainant, it can be said that the man's higher pay would have been justified on the basis of his job duties had he not suffered from illness. The man's illness is the factor distinguishing his case from that of the woman. Thus in *Outlook Supplies Ltd* v. *Parry*,[37] the male comparator had been relieved of part of his additional and more responsible duties due to ill health and the personal protection of his rate was upheld.

In contrast, where the man was employed on work of equal or lesser value to that performed by the woman prior to the occurrence which led to the red circle being formed, the existence of the red circle is really an irrelevancy. Unless the man's higher pay was justified for some other reason before the formation of the red circle, the effect of the red circle will simply be to protect and perpetuate the unjustified inequality.

Using this analysis and taking the three kinds of situations set out above, it can be seen that there is a conceptual distinction between red circles resulting from changes to the employee or to his job on the one hand, and changes resulting from job evaluation or re-grading on the other hand. In the former cases, provided there is no taint of sex discrimination and there were valid reasons for paying the man more before the formation of the red circle, a red circle defence should be acceptable.

The latter situation, however, is characterised by the absence of tangible change either in relation to the job or the job-holder and simply involves a change in how the job is perceived. Can this in itself justify higher pay by protecting the man's rate? We would suggest that the Regulations cannot be viewed as permitting a woman's right to equal pay for work which has been held to be of equal value to be defeated simply because the man has been in receipt of higher pay, even if there is no evidence that sex discrimination has contributed to protection of the man's rate. If a present inequality in pay can be justified simply on the basis of a past inequality, the Act would have a very limited application indeed. That the man has been paid more in the past cannot be considered of sufficient materiality to justify a difference in pay, particularly since any hardship to the man resulting from a reduction in his pay can be obviated by increasing the woman's pay instead.[38]

GRADING DIFFERENCES

Whether it is a defence under s.1(3) for an employer to argue that a difference in pay between workers employed on work of equal value arises out of the operation of a grading scheme, presents similar issues to those raised in our discussion of red circle defences.

In a series of cases, the courts have been willing to accept pay differentials for employees on like work or work rated as equivalent which have been based on industry-wide or nationally-negotiated grading systems. Thus, in *Waddington v. Leicester Council for Voluntary Services*, the EAT held:

Where men and women are employed on like work, and the

> variation is in the rate of remuneration, and the remuneration is fixed in accordance with nationally, or widely, negotiated wage scales, it would seem to us that there will usually be a strong case for saying that the case falls within subsection (3). There the variation very likely is genuinely due to a material difference other than a difference of sex, viz: that the man and the woman have been placed in different wage scales, or at different points in the same scale. In other words the difference is due to a matter of grading.[39]

Such a construction of the statute is understandable in that it avoids the problems which would ensue if a claim in such circumstances were upheld. This was very much on the EAT's mind in *Waddington*:

> Suppose a man and a woman are doing like work, each being paid in accordance with his place in different scales, which have become out of phase. If a woman (or a man) succeeds in a claim under the Equal Pay Act 1970, all the other men (or women) employed on like work with her (or him) will have a claim based on the variation between his salary (or her) and her (or his) adjusted salary. There will be a proliferation of competing claims, and the Industrial Tribunal will have to revise the wage scales – which is not its function.

Expediency is the principal merit in the reasoning of this line of cases, and it is suggested that on a proper construction of the statute, the reasoning is insupportable. In essence, these cases permit the employer's perception of the different values attached to the work of the man and the woman, as reflected in their different grading, to constitute a valid defence. At least for the purposes of the new Regulations, it is suggested that such a defence cannot be acceptable since it is precisely the question of whether the work was of equal value which has been adjudicated. As with red circle cases, that the employer genuinely thought the work unequal should not be regarded as a sufficient defence under a correct interpretation of the statute. To permit a defence simply on the basis that the grading system is non-discriminatory is tantamount to permitting a defence on the basis that the employer has acted in good faith in paying unequal pay.

SERVICE PAYMENTS

At first sight, additional payments for additional service appear to provide a typical example of a material factor which would normally prove an acceptable defence under the new Regulations. They have been so regarded by the courts in dealing with like work and work rated as equivalent claims.[40]

Where both groups in question receive service payments, the justification is that the complainant will get the additional payment when she achieves the requisite service. An argument could be mounted that service pay indirectly discriminates against women because of their shorter average service.[41] However, the practical consequences which would ensue make the chance of a successful challenge to a *bona fide* service-based system remote. In an analogous case under the Sex Discrimination Act, the EAT went out of its way to offer the view that seniority-based redundancy selection procedures would be regarded as acceptable.[42] Thus, we would anticipate that an employer with a common-or-garden service-based incremental pay scheme applying to all relevant groups would normally be able to justify a differential under s.1(3).[43]

Equal value claims, however, as we noted at the beginning of this chapter, may present a new issue in so far as they may entail comparisons between a group of workers without a service payment scheme and a group with service payments, e.g. a manual worker making a comparison with a clerical worker of the opposite sex. In such circumstances, it is not the difference in service which is the factor explaining the pay differential. Both employees may have equal service. The variation is due to a difference in compensation policies. This raises very different questions.

The first issue of importance is whether the difference in compensation policies is sexually discriminatory. If it is a group of women manual workers, for example, making the claim and no manual workers receive service increments, the reason for the differential is unlikely to be sex-based, since there will be men in similar circumstances who do not receive service increments. Even so, that does not mean that the claim will not succeed in part. The defence should apply only to that portion of the differential between the groups which is attributable to the service payment scheme and the equality clause should apply to basic rates (or if the service element is not expressed discretely, by discounting for it such as was recommended by the EAT in the case of additional payment for weekend working in *Electrolux Ltd* v. *Hutchinson and others*).[44] This, it should be emphasised, is a principle which also applies to other potential material factor defences under the Regulations and it follows from this general proposition that *all* of the variation must be explainable in terms of the material factor.

In any event, it must be asked whether the difference in compensation policies is a 'material factor' and, in particular, why one group receives service increments and not the other. If the answer is the importance of ensuring experienced workers in the one job, it can be argued that the need for experience has already been taken into account in determining whether the jobs were of equal value. To, in effect, count it twice would be tantamount to arguing that a man employed on work of equal value should be paid more because his job requires more effort.

QUALIFICATIONS AND EXPERIENCE

Differences in pay genuinely based on academic or professional qualifications present some of the same problems as differences based on service. If the qualifications are needed for the job, they will have been taken into account in determining whether the jobs are of equal value.

Women, on average, as we saw in Chapter 2, have fewer formal qualifications than men, so additional payments for qualifications would usually have an adverse impact upon women. If so, if the guidance of *Jenkins* v. *Kingsgate No. 2* is followed,[45] the employer at the least will be asked to show the business objective which the additional payment purports to achieve. Given that the qualifications are not required for the job being done, this may not be all that easy. Realistically, though, it is somehow difficult to imagine British courts striking down additional payments for qualifications if they are part of a well-defined payment system.

There are also disparate treatment questions which may arise out of qualifications payments that have not emerged under the 1970 Act. If there is additional compensation for extra qualifications in the men's jobs but not in the women's jobs, that raises an inference of discrimination.

Additional payments for experience with other employers raises other issues because it rarely forms part of an overall payment system and is more likely to be offered as a justification for higher pay in respect of particular individuals. In most cases, it is difficult to see past experience with other firms as a valid justification in itself for unequal pay. Where past experience is relevant, it would be expected that differences in experience would be reflected in differences in work performed and that the employee with greater experience would be performing work of greater value. Alternatively, the employee will be performing work of equal value but doing it better so that higher pay will be justified on grounds of performance or merit and not experience *per se*. In many jobs of an unskilled or semi-skilled nature, the requisite level of experience is quickly reached. The courts should be wary of purported differences in experience being used as a guise for market forces with the man's alleged experience being a pretext for the need to match his previous salary. Where experience is not directly reflected in the work undertaken or in performance, the employer should be required to show why it justifies higher pay. This was the approach taken by the Northern Ireland Court of Appeal in *Brunt* v. *The Northern Ireland Electricity Service*,[46] where the man was offered a starting salary of £150 per annum more than the applicant for the same work. The Court of Appeal pointed out that there was no 'sign that his longer experience in the world and at work (though not experience of, or necessarily fitting him for, the type of work offered by the respondents) had any bearing on the efficiency with which he might be expected to carry out his duties or on his probable general usefulness as an employee of the respondents'.

TRAINING SCHEME

That the man employed on work of equal value with whom the woman is claiming equality is undergoing training for a higher position may constitute a justification for higher pay under s.1(3). However, more should be required than a conclusory assertion that the man is being trained for a different position. The EAT's decision in *Redland Roof Tiles Ltd* v. *Harper*[47] suggests that there should be evidence of a formal training scheme. In that case, rejecting an appeal against an Industrial Tribunal's finding that a female clerk was entitled to equal pay with a Mr Bartin, said to be a trainee manager, the EAT commented: 'There was no evidence there of any organised scheme for trainee managers under which Mr Bartin was operating. The sort of thing we have in mind is the kind of case where a man is engaged as a trainee manager, perhaps being paid a little more than those alongside whom he is working, and who moves from department to department, or office to office, to gain experience over the entire field in which eventually he hopes to become a manager.'

MERIT PAY

Merit or performance payments are a valid reason for unequal pay. Where an employer is justifying a differential on grounds of differences in performance, the proper focus of inquiry under s.1(3) is whether the assessment was *bona fide* and free of sex bias.

A subjective merit assessment may be prone to bias either in intent or effect. But the mere fact that assessments are made subjectively will not invalidate their results for the purposes of s.1(3). As Lord Justice Geoffrey Lane pointed out in *National Vulcan Engineering Insurance Co Ltd* v. *Wade*, 'it is not for the Tribunal to examine the employers' system with the object of seeing whether it is operating efficiently or even fairly'. Rather, as Lord Justice Ormrod put it in the same case, it is only if the scheme conceals 'an underlying sex discrimination in rates of pay' that it will not satisfy the requirements of s.1(3).[48]

LOCATION OF WORK

S.1(6) of the Equal Pay Act permits comparisons to be made between employees in different establishments if 'common terms and conditions of employment are observed either generally or for employees of the relevant classes'. But even where a claim across establishments falls within s.1(6) and there is a finding of work of equal value, that the employees work in different geographical locations may serve as a defence under s.1(3). This is the effect of the EAT's decision in *NAAFI* v. *Varley*,[49] where a difference in weekly hours of work between employees in Nottingham and London was held to be due to a geographical difference which was not sex-based.

As with other material factor defences, the chances of an argument based on location of work succeeding will be considerably influenced by whether the groups in question are segregated by sex or whether the difference in terms and conditions applies to men as well as women in both locations. In the *NAAFI* case, both men and women in Nottingham worked a 37-hour week and both men and women employed in London worked a 36½-hour week, and there was no suggestion that the difference in hours was sexually based. Similar reasoning would permit an employer to justify paying all workers in London more than their provincial counterparts. On the other hand, if the work being compared in one location was performed only by men and in the other location was performed only by women, it would suggest in the absence of further evidence that the distinguishing factor was the sex of the workers rather than where they worked.

DIFFERENCES IN TIME WORKED

Differences in the time of day during which work is performed have been held not to constitute a difference which can be taken into account for the purpose of determining whether two jobs are the same or broadly similar.[50] It can be anticipated that the mere fact that one employee works days and the other nights will not be regarded as a factor in determining under the new Regulations whether their work is of equal value.

Where employees are compensated for the extra burden of working unsocial hours by a separate shift premium, there is no doubt that this is permissible. More complicated issues arise where a shift supplement is built into basic rates or where there is an element in basic rates for an agreement to work shifts as well as a premium when shifts are actually worked, In either case, where shiftworking is not reflected in a discrete element in the basic rates, it raises the difficult question of whether all of the variation in pay is due to the difference in time worked. The EAT's decision in *National Coal Board* v. *Sherwin and Spruce* is authority for the proposition that shiftworking or a willingness to work shifts does not justify a differential in basic rates of unlimited proportions. This case implicitly rejected the simplistic view that once a material difference – e.g. shiftworking – has been established, the defence under s.1(3) has been proved. If the day shift is composed entirely of women and the night shift of men, the origins of the differential may be tainted by sex discrimination. It may be asked, for example, whether the differential would have been the same if men were employed on the day shift. The correct approach, it is suggested, is that if part of the differential is justified because of the need to attract and retain shift workers, the rates should be equalised after making an allowance for the differential which the Industrial Tribunal thinks reasonable in the circumstances to compensate for shiftworking. Only if the Tribunal thinks that the entire differential is attributable to shiftworking and that none of the differential is attributable, either directly or indirectly, to sex discrimination, should the need to fill shift posts prove a complete defence under s.1(3).

HOURS OF WORK

Whether an employer is entitled to pay a lower hourly rate to part-time workers or otherwise treat them less favourably than full-time workers of the opposite sex was the issue considered by the European Court of Justice in *Jenkins* v. *Kingsgate (Clothing Productions) Ltd* and subsequently by the EAT in *Jenkins No. 2*. The European Court's decision established that a differential in pay between women and men doing equal work cannot be justified simply by showing that the women are part-time workers. *Jenkins No. 2*, as we have noted, laid down the principle that, where the part-time workers are mainly women, to fall within s.1(3) an employer must show that the lower pay for part-time workers is in fact reasonably necessary in order to obtain some result (other than cheap female labour) which the employer desires for economic or other reasons. Reducing absenteeism and obtaining the maximum utilisation of plant were mentioned by the EAT as objectives which might justify lower pay for part-time workers. In a significant passage, however, the EAT added: 'We must emphasise that this question arises only if the employer proves that the differential in pay *in fact* produces these results: it does not deal with the case where the employer *intends* to produce these results without showing that the results are in fact produced.' We suggested above that as a general statement of principle, this dictum is unlikely to withstand the tests of time. But in the case of differences between part-time workers and full-time workers employed on work of equal value, it will be the relevant legal authority unless or until it is overruled.

REMEDIES

If the work being compared is found to be of equal value, and the employer has not justified the difference in pay in terms of s.1(3)(b), the complainant will succeed. The Industrial Tribunal will award arrears of remuneration, the difference between what the applicant earned and what her comparator earned. Under s.2(5) of the Equal Pay Act, the successful claimant is entitled to up to two years' back pay from the date the proceedings were instituted. However, since the right to bring an equal value claim arose only with effect from 1 January 1984 and is not retrospective, it will not be until 1 January 1986 that successful applicants will be able to get arrears of pay for the full two-year maximum period.

The Industrial Tribunal will also declare that the equality clause deemed to be included in the applicant's contract of employment has been contravened. Bear in mind that s.1(2) of the Act states in terms that 'an equality clause is a provision which relates to terms (whether concerned with pay or not) of a contract under which a woman is employed'. As we indicated in Chapter 3, unless the employer has argued and the Tribunal has accepted that there is a term of the woman's contract which should not, by reason of s.1(3), be equalised, each and every term of the woman's contract will be modified by law so as to accord with the contract of her male comparator. Such a change in contractual rights will take place in spite of the fact that those terms do not relate to basic pay or to pay at all, notwithstanding that hitherto the contracts of the employees concerned have been determined by different collective agreements or remuneration policies. For this reason, whatever else it achieves, equal pay for work of equal value should prove to be a great stimulus to eliminating status distinctions between grades of workers.

NOTES

1. Per Lord Justice Geoffrey Lane in the analogous pre-amendment case of *National Vulcan Engineering Insurance Group Ltd* v. *Wade* [1978] IRLR 225 CA.
2. It must be admitted that the case law under the Equal Pay Act is not consistent and that the courts, in attempting to ensure that equal pay law does not become 'too legalistic', have sometimes adopted what can only be described as a simplistic approach to s.1(3). Thus, in *Methven and Musiolik* v. *Cow Industrial Polymers Ltd* [1980] IRLR 289 CA, the Court of Appeal accepted a three-part test suggested by counsel: '(1) Was there a variation between the woman's contract and the man's? (2) Was there a material difference (other than difference of sex) between her case and his? Have the employers proved on the balance of probabilities that the variation in wages was due to the material difference?'

3. [1978] IRLR 122. But see *Boyle* v. *Tennant Caledonian Breweries* [1978] IRLR 321. The view of the Court of Appeal in the *Methven* case that s.1(3) simply involves determining whether 'the employers proved on the balance of probabilities that the variation in wages was due to the material difference' is also not in accord with this approach. In that case, the court accepted the question as being one of 'causation' and 'like all questions of causation', it was 'a question of fact'.
4. *Jenkins* v. *Kingsgate (Clothing Productions) Ltd* [1981] IRLR 228.
5. [1981] IRLR 388.
6. [1978] IRLR 361.
7. *National Coal Board* v. *Sherwin and Spruce* [1978] IRLR 122.
8. Per Lord Denning, Master of the Rolls.
9. The case has also been limited by subsequent decisions such as *Farthing and others* v. *Ministry of Defence* [1980] IRLR 402 CA, *Albion Shipping Agency* v. *Arnold* [1981] IRLR 520 and *Rainey* v. *Greater Glasgow Health Board Eastern District* [1984] IRLR 88 EAT.
10. Such a standard was adopted by the Ninth Circuit Court of Appeals in America in the recent pay discrimination case of *Kouba* v. *Allstate Insurance Co* (1982) 30 FEP Cases 57.

    The Equal Pay Act concerns business practices. It would be nonsensical to sanction the use of a factor that rests on some consideration unrelated to business. An employer thus cannot use a factor which causes a wage differential between male and female employees absent an acceptable business reason . . . A pragmatic standard, which protects against abuse, yet accommodates employer discretion, is that the employer must use the factor reasonably in light of the employer's stated purpose as well as its other practices.
11. Per Lord Justice Bridge [1978] IRLR 263.
12. It does not accord, however, with a literal reading of the statutory language. Part of the concept of indirect discrimination is that the direct cause of the difference in treatment is not the difference of sex but is a reason, neutral on its face, having a disproportionate impact.
13. Thus Lord Gowrie pointed out in the Lords' debate on the Regulations: 'the defence is drafted in such a way that the employer can never succeed with an argument which rests on there being a difference of sex . . . It has never been suggested that the existing material difference defence allowed an employer to argue matters grounded in sex, whether directly or indirectly, and so I fail to see why the new test is open to that charge.' (*Hansard*, House of Lords, 5.12.83, col. 925.)
14. The EAT in *Jenkins No. 2* seems to have taken the view that intentional indirect discrimination is not justifiable, at least for the purposes of s.1(3): 'If the Industrial Tribunal finds that the employers intended to discriminate against women by paying part-time workers less, the employers cannot succeed under s.1(3).' Such an approach still requires a showing of disparate impact, however.

    It is possible to draw a distinction between intentional and unintentional indirect discrimination, but it is not the one drawn by the EAT. International indirect discrimination may be regarded as being where the employer has a genuine neutral purpose but knows that the effect of his efforts to achieve that purpose have a disparate impact on women. Unintentional indirect discrimination may be equated with unknowing indirect discrimination.

15. This is what makes the distinction drawn in *Jenkins No. 2* virtually meaningless. No sensible employer would attempt to defend 'overt' discrimination on grounds of sex. Nor is it likely that an employer will own up to stereotyped assumptions which may have motivated him – such as that women work for 'pin money' or that men are 'breadwinners'.
16. This has been held in terms under American legislation by the US Supreme Court in *International Brotherhood of Teamsters* v. *United States* (1977) 431 US 324.
17. *Holland* v. *Edwards* NY CA (1954) 307 NY 38. As I pointed out in 'The Law of Sexual Harassment at Work', *Industrial Law Journal*, March 1983, the frequently used term 'direct discrimination' to characterise less favourable treatment on grounds of sex is a misnomer. Such discrimination is usually anything but direct.
18. 1980 IRLR 193 NICA.
19. *Ojutiku and Oburoni* v. *Manpower Services Commission* [1982] IRLR 418. Lord Justice Stephenson adopted a standard close to the 'reasonable necessity' test in *Jenkins No. 2*. He suggested that the party applying the discriminatory condition must prove it to be justifiable balancing its discriminatory effect against the discriminator's need for it – with that 'need' being 'what is reasonably needed by the party who applies the condition'.
20. [1982] IRLR 482.
21. Complicating the picture even further is the fact that the EAT in *Jenkins No. 2* assumed that it was going further than the European Court required: 'It seems to us right that we should construe the Equal Pay Act 1970 as requiring any difference in pay to be objectively justified even if this confers on employees greater rights than they would enjoy under Article 119 of the Treaty.'
22. Taken to its logical conclusion, a test requiring the employer to show that the variation was in fact reasonably necessary to achieve his purpose, would require the employer to show evidence that his purpose has in fact been achieved and was not simply still an aspiration; that it was the variation in pay that was responsible for the purpose being achieved and, by implication, that it could not have been achieved had there not been the variation in pay; and that there was no other way to achieve the objective without the variation in pay. To take the example of service increments mentioned above, which may have the effect of indirectly discriminating against women since they on average have shorter service, this would require statistics showing that service increments produce lower turnover and, presumably, some evidence that without the service increments turnover would be higher. Few, if any, employers are likely to be able to produce such evidence.

23. *Hansard*, House of Commons, 20.7.83, col. 486.
24. *Hansard*, House of Lords, 5.22.83, col. 884.
25. Just as employment decisions may not be predicated on accurate generalisations about women or on customer preference, both of which may be efficient from the employer's standpoint. 'Equal Pay, Comparable Work, and Job Evaluation', *Yale Law Journal*, vol. 90, 1981, p. 633.
26. *Marshall* v. *J. L. Hudson* [DC Mich] (1979) 19 EPD @ 9108.
27. See 'Equal Pay for Comparable Work', *Harvard Civil Rights-Civil Liberties Law Review*, vol. 15, 1980, p. 475.
28. This was the principle set out by the US Supreme Court in the equal pay case of *Corning Glass Works* v. *Brennan* (1974) 9 FEP Cases 919, where it was argued that market forces were a 'factor other than sex' within the meaning of the exceptions to the American statute. In a decision which may be of persuasive authority for the interpretation of the UK Regulations, the Supreme Court said:

    > The differential arose simply because men would not work at the low rates paid women inspectors, and it reflected a job market in which Corning could pay women less than men for the same work. That the Company took advantage of such a situation may be understandable as a matter of economics, but its differential nevertheless became illegal once Congress enacted into law the principle of equal pay for equal work.

    Note that the new language of s.1(3) introduces for the first time the words 'factor which is not the difference of sex', virtually identical with the language construed by the Supreme Court.
29. It is important, in this context, to focus in on what the issue of market forces involves. Sensible proponents of equal pay for work of equal value are not trying to preclude the use of the market as a reference point for the determination of wages. The question is whether the existence of separate labour markets for men and women should be allowed to result in men getting higher pay for work of equal value. If a female senior secretary and a male lathe operator are found to be employed on work of equal value, there is nothing to stop the employer from setting the rates of pay on the basis of the market rate for lathe operators. The only issue which arises under the new Regulations is whether he is entitled to take the further step of paying the senior secretaries less than that rate because sufficient women can be attracted at a lower salary.

    Similarly, there is a vital distinction between using the market to position a firm's wage structure as a whole and using the market to determine the rates of pay for individual jobs. In a sense, it is a question of which process is undertaken first. If a firm surveys the market for men's and women's jobs and positions its own wages accordingly, that has the effect of translating any discrimination in the market into the wage structure of the firm. There is nothing discriminatory, however, in aligning the women's jobs with the men's through a grading system and evaluation and using the market rates for the men's jobs as the key for positioning the wage structure as a whole. If this is done, the pay for the women's jobs will be determined according to the market rate for the men's jobs. Of course, the obvious corollary is that women will receive higher pay for their jobs than the market dictates.

30. In the recent American equal pay case of *Winkes* v. *Brown University* [DC RI] (1983) 32 FEP Cases 1041, it was held that in order to show a successful market force defence, 'at a minimum . . . the defendant institution must have studied the going market rates of particular disciplines and be prepared to pay the same dollar amount to a qualified man or woman'. In this case, the employer's defence was rejected where 'no evidence was presented which would indicate what the job market was like . . . No availability of positions, estimated applicant pools or salary ranges of various institutions were discussed'. See also *Marshall* v. *Georgia Southwestern College* [DC Ga] (1980) 23 FEP Cases 451: 'Any credibility that the market force defense might have is diminished by the fact that those charged with hiring did not inform themselves of the market rates of particular expertise, experience or skill.'
31. Townshend-Smith, *Modern Law Review*, vol. 47: 2, March 1984, surely exaggerates the case, however, in suggesting that 'in the majority of cases' such evidence 'would be almost impossible to produce'.
32. Lisa L. Shapiro, 'Sex-Based Wage Discrimination: One Step Beyond The Equal Pay Act', *Hofstra Law Review*, vol. 9, 1981, p. 1526.
33. See Christopher McCrudden, 'Equal Pay for Work of Equal Value: the Equal Pay (Amendment) Regulations 1983', *The Industrial Law Journal*, vol. 12, no. 4, December 1983. See also *Industrial Relations Review & Report*, no. 315; Townshend-Smith, *Modern Law Review*, vol. 47: 2, March 1984.
34. Although this issue was originally raised by McCrudden, I have eschewed his example of female typists and male engineers since it seems doubtful whether such jobs would be found to be of equal value.
35. That the employer in such circumstances may be regarded as merely acceding to the union's discriminatory pressure does not absolve him of the legal consequence any more than he would be absolved if the union threatened to strike if he hired a black man. On this point, McCrudden's analysis lacks his customary incisiveness and clarity of thought. He seems to place great weight on the question of whether the employer 'should be regarded as jointly responsible' with the union for the higher wages in the men's jobs since the choice as to how to divide the wage packet is 'not made by unions alone'. Many may feel that this is a proposition so self-evident as scarcely to need stating and it is hardly conceivable that a Tribunal would accept that an employer bore no responsibility for the wage structure in his firm.
36. [1977] IRLR 123. The principle has been endorsed by the Court of Appeal in *E. Coomes (Holdings) Ltd* v. *Shields* and followed by the EAT in subsequent cases.

37. [1978] IRLR 12 EAT.
38. The cost of implementing equal pay (in this case, by raising the woman's rates rather than lowering the man's rates) should not be regarded as a relevant factor.
39. [1977] IRLR 32. Those remarks were quoted with approval by Lord Denning in *Pointon* v. *The University of Sussex* [1979] IRLR 119 CA, who suggested 'the simple answer to the whole of this case is that a grading on national scales does not infringe the Act in the least so long as it is operated irrespective of sex'. However, the *Pointon* case involved a very different issue – whether a salary structure based on qualifications and experience was discriminatory, rather than, as in *Waddington*, a grading system which evaluated job duties. See also *Graviner Ltd* v. *Hughes* (12.7.78, EAT No: 46/78) and *England* v. *The London Borough of Bromley* (5.4.77; EAT No: 496/77).
40. See *Capper Pass Ltd* v. *Lawton* [1976] IRLR 366 EAT, *Fletcher* v. *Clay Cross (Quarry Services) Ltd.*
41. An incremental scheme based on cumulative, as opposed to continuous, service with the firm would have less of an adverse impact upon women.
42. *Clarke* v. *Eley (IMI Kynoch) Ltd.*
43. Differences in service, however, cannot be used as an after-the-fact rationalisation of pay discrimination. The employer must advance some evidence to show that the additional payment genuinely was made to the man in respect of his additional service. In *Honeywell Ltd* v. *Scott* (2.12.77; EAT No: 481/77), the employers' defence that the complainant's male comparator had longer service was rejected when it was shown that the complainant was also paid less than another man who had the same service as she. The EAT said: 'If an employer intends to rely upon length of service as a material difference then it is, in our opinion, incumbent upon him at least to introduce some evidence as to how the particular differences came about.' See, however, *Boyle* v. *Tennant Caledonian Breweries Ltd* [1978] IRLR 321, in which the EAT refused to allow an appeal based on the employer's failure to quantify with precision the element of the man's pay attributable to his longer service.
44. [1976] IRLR 410.
45. *Jenkins* makes the early decision in *Murray* v. *Lothian Regional Council* (8.12.76; EAT No: 530/76) on this point questionable. In that case, the EAT overruled an Industrial Tribunal which did not regard possession of an honours degree as a valid basis for higher pay for teachers employed on equal work. The Industrial Tribunal held that 'the difference between an honours degree and an ordinary degree had no bearing on the actual work done'. According to the EAT, however, 'both parties are employed in a college of education, both are teachers, and both are to be remunerated in accordance with the recognised salary structure. If that provides for a higher rate of pay for an honours graduate that is in our view a genuine and material variation which is unrelated to sex'.

46. 21.3.79. See also the EAT's decision in *ARW Transformers Ltd* v. *Cupples* [1977] IRLR 228.
47. 26.11.76; EAT No: 233/76.
48. [1978] IRLR 225 CA. In this case, there was no evidence that the scheme was being used as a pretext for discrimination and there was positive evidence that both men and women had received high personal assessments and low personal assessments, so that the scheme was not discriminatory in effect.
49. [1976] IRLR 408.
50. *Dugdale* v. *Kraft Foods Ltd* [1976] IRLR 368 EAT.

Appendix I: The Equal Pay (Amendment) Regulations 1983 – S.I. 1983 No. 1794

Citation, commencement and extent

1.—(1) These Regulations may be cited as the Equal Pay (Amendment) Regulations 1983.

(2) These Regulations shall come into operation on 1st January 1984.

(3) These Regulations do not extend to Northern Ireland.

New form of equality clause

2.—(1) In subsection (2) of section 1 of the Equal Pay Act 1970 (equality clauses to be implied into contracts of employment), after paragraph *(b)* there shall be inserted the following paragraph:—

"*(c)* where a woman is employed on work which, not being work in relation to which paragraph *(a)* or *(b)* above applies, is, in terms of the demands made on her (for instance under such headings as effort, skill and decision), of equal value to that of a man in the same employment—

(i) if (apart from the equality clause) any term of the woman's contract is or becomes less favourable to the woman than a term of a similar kind in the contract under which that man is employed, that term of the woman's contract shall be treated as so modified as not to be less favourable, and

(ii) if (apart from the equality clause) at any time the woman's contract does not include a term corresponding to a term benefiting that man included in the contract under which he is employed, the woman's contract shall be treated as including such a term.".

(2) For subsection (3) of the said section 1 (defence of genuine material difference) there shall be substituted the following subsection:—

"(3) An equality clause shall not operate in relation to a variation between the woman's contract and the man's contract if the employer proves that the variation is genuinely due to a material factor which is not the difference of sex and that factor—

(*a*) in the case of an equality clause falling within subsection (2)(*a*) or (*b*) above, must be a material difference between the woman's case and the man's; and

(*b*) in the case of an equality clause falling within subsection (2)(*c*) above, may be such a material difference.".

Procedure before industrial tribunal

3.—(1) After section 2 of the said Act of 1970 (disputes as to, and enforcement of, requirement of equal treatment), there shall be inserted the following section:—

"Procedure before tribunal in certain cases.

2A.—(1) Where on a complaint or reference made to an industrial tribunal under section 2 above, a dispute arises as to whether any work is of equal value as mentioned in section 1(2)(*c*) above the tribunal shall not determine that question unless—

(*a*) it is satisfied that there are no reasonable grounds for determining that the work is of equal value as so mentioned; or

(*b*) it has required a member of the panel of independent experts to prepare a report with respect to that question and has received that report.

(2) Without prejudice to the generality of paragraph (*a*) of subsection (1) above, there shall be taken, for the purposes of that paragraph, to be no reasonable grounds for determining that the work of a woman is of equal value as mentioned in section 1(2)(*c*) above if—

(*a*) that work and the work of the man in question have been given different values on a study such as is mentioned in section 1(5) above; and

(*b*) there are no reasonable grounds for determining that the evaluation contained in the study was (within the meaning of subsection (3) below) made on a system which discriminates on grounds of sex.

(3) An evaluation contained in a study such as is mentioned in section 1(5) above is made on a system which discriminates on grounds of sex where a difference, or coincidence, between values set by that system on different demands under the same or different headings is not justifiable irrespective of the sex of the person on whom those demands are made.

(4) In paragraph (*b*) of subsection (1) above the reference to a member of the panel of independent experts is a reference to a person who is for the time being designated by the Advisory, Conciliation and Arbitration Service for the purposes of that paragraph as such a member, being neither a member of the Council of that Service nor one of its officers or servants.".

(2) Accordingly, in subsection (13) of section 1 of the said Act of 1970 (application in relation to men as well as to women), for the words "section 2" there shall be substituted the words "sections 2 and 2A".

(3) In paragraph 1(2) of Schedule 9 to the Employment Protection (Consolidation) Act 1978 (regulations with respect to proceedings before industrial tribunals), after paragraph (g) there shall be inserted the following paragraph:—

"*(ga)* for authorising an industrial tribunal to require persons to furnish information and produce documents to a person required for the purposes of section 2A(1)*(b)* of the Equal Pay Act 1970 to prepare a report;";

and, accordingly, in paragraph 1(7) of that Schedule (offences for failure to comply with requirements imposed by the regulations), after the words "sub-paragraph (2)*(d)* " there shall be inserted the words "or *(ga)* ".

(4) In paragraph 10 of the said Schedule 9 (remuneration etc. for members of industrial tribunals and for assessors and other persons), after the word "tribunals", in the second place where it occurs, there shall be inserted the words "and to any persons required for the purposes of section 2A(1)*(b)* of the Equal Pay Act 1970 to prepare reports'.

Signed by order of the Secretary of State.

Appendix II: Sections 1 and 2 of the Equal Pay Act 1970 as amended by Equal Pay (Amendment) Regulations 1983 (S.I. 1983 No.1794)

The amendments are printed in italics.

1. (1) If the terms of a contract under which a woman is employed at an establishment in Great Britain do not include (directly or by reference to a collective agreement or otherwise) an equality clause they shall be deemed to include one.

(2) An equality clause is a provision which relates to terms (whether concerned with pay or not) of a contract under which a woman is employed (the "woman's contract", and has the effect that

(a) where the woman is employed on like work with a man in the same employment

(i) if (apart from the equality clause) any term of the woman's contract is or becomes less favourable to the woman than a term of a similar kind in the contract under which that man is employed, that term of the woman's contract shall be treated as so modified as not to be less favourable, and

(ii) if (apart from the equality clause) at any time the woman's contract does not include a term corresponding to a term benefiting that man included in the contract under which he is employed, the woman's contract shall be treated as including such a term;

(b) where the woman is employed on work rated as equivalent with that of a man in the same employment

(i) if (apart from the equality clause) any term of the woman's contract determined by the rating of the work is or becomes less favourable to the woman than a term of a similar kind in the contract under which that man is employed, that term of the woman's contract shall be treated as so modified as not to be less favourable, and

(ii) if (apart from the equality clause) at any time the woman's contract does not include a term corresponding to a term benefiting that man included in the contract under which he is employed and determined by the rating of the work, the woman's contract shall be treated as including such a term.

(c) where a woman is employed on work which, not being work in relation to which paragraph (a) or (b) above applies, is, in terms of the demands made on her (for instance under such headings as effort, skill and decision), of equal value to that of a man in the same employment

(i) if (apart from the equality clause) any term of the woman's contract is or becomes less favourable to the woman than a term of a similar kind in the contract under which that man is employed, that term of the woman's contract shall be treated as so modified as not to be less favourable, and

(ii) if (apart from the equality clause) at any time the woman's contract does not include a term corresponding to a term benefiting that man included in the contract under which he is employed, the woman's contract shall be treated as including such a term.

(3) An equality clause shall not operate in relation to a variation between the woman's contract and the man's contract if the employer proves that the variation is genuinely due to a material factor which is not the difference of sex and that factor

(a) in the case of an equality clause falling within subsection (2)(a) or (b) above, must be a material difference between the woman's case and the man's; and

(b) in the case of an equality clause falling within subsection (2)(c) above, may be such a material difference.

(4) A woman is to be regarded as employed on like work with men if, but only if, her work and theirs is of the same or a broadly similar nature, and the differences (if any) between the things she does and the things they do are not of practical importance in relation to terms and conditions of employment; and accordingly in comparing her work with theirs regard shall be had to the frequency or otherwise with which any such differences occur in practice as well as to the nature and extent of the differences.

(5) A woman is to be regarded as employed on work rated as equivalent

with that of any men if, but only if, her job and their job have been given an equal value in terms of the demand made on a worker under various headings (for instance effort, skill, decision), on a study undertaken with a view to evaluating in those terms the jobs to be done by all or any of the employees in an undertaking or group of undertakings, or would have been given an equal value but for the evaluation being made on a system setting different values for men and women on the same demand under any heading.

(6) Subject to the following subsections, for purposes of this section

(a) "employed" means employed under a contract of service or of apprenticeship or a contract personally to execute any work or labour, and related expressions shall be construed accordingly.

(c) two employers are to be treated as associated if one is a company of which the other (directly or indirectly) has control of if both are companies of which a third person (directly or indirectly) has control,

and men shall be treated as in the same employment with a woman if they are men employed by her employer or any associated employer at the same establishment or at establishments in Great Britain which include that one and at which common terms and conditions of employment are observed either generally or for employees of the relevant classes.

(8) This section shall apply to

(a) service for purposes of a Minister of the Crown or government department, other than service of a person holding a statutory office, or

(b) service on behalf of the Crown for purposes of a person as it applies to employment by a private person,

and shall so apply as if references to a contract of employment included references to the terms of service.

(9) Subsection (8) does not apply in relation to service in –

(a) the naval, military or air forces of the Crown, or
(b) any women's service administered by the Defence Council.

(10) In this section "statutory body" means a body set up by or in pursuance of an enactment, and "statutory office" means an office so set up; and service "for purposes of" a Minister of the Crown or government department does not include service in any office in Schedule 2 (Ministerial offices) to the House of Commons Disqualification Act 1975 as for the time being in force.

(11) For the purposes of this Act it is immaterial whether the law which

(apart from this subsection) is the proper law of a contract is the law of any part of the United Kingdom or not.

(12) In this Act "Great Britain" includes such of the territorial waters of the United Kingdom as are adjacent to Great Britain.

(13) Provisions of this section and section 2 and 2A below framed with reference to women and their treatment relative to men are to be read as applying equally in a converse case to men and their treatment relative to women.

2. (1) Any claim in respect of the contravention of a term modified or included by virtue of an equality clause, including a claim for arrears of remuneration or damages in respect of the contravention, may be presented by way of a complaint to an industrial tribunal.

(1A) Where a dispute arises in relation to the effect of an equality clause the employer may apply to an industrial tribunal for an order declaring the rights of the employer and the employee in relation to the matter in question.

(2) Where it appears to the Secretary of State that there may be a question whether the employer of any women is or has been contravening a term modified or included by virtue of their equality clauses, but that it is not reasonable to expect them to take steps to have the question determined, the question may be referred by him as respects all or any of them to an industrial tribunal and shall be dealt with as if the reference were of a claim by the women or woman against the employer.

(3) Where it appears to the court in which any proceedings are pending that a claim or counterclaim in respect of the operation of an equality clause could more conveniently be disposed of separately by an industrial tribunal, the court may direct that the claim or counterclaim shall be struck out; and (without prejudice to the foregoing) where in proceedings before any court a question arises as to the operation of an equality clause, the court may on the application of any party to the proceedings or otherwise refer that question, or direct it to be referred by a party to the proceedings, to an industrial tribunal for determination by the tribunal, and may stay or sist the proceedings in the meantime.

(4) No claim in respect of the operation of an equality clause relating to a woman's employment shall be referred to an industrial tribunal otherwise than by virtue of subsection (3) above, if she has not been employed in the employment within the six months preceding the date of the reference.

(5) A woman shall not be entitled, in proceedings brought in respect of a failure to comply with an equality clause (including proceedings before an industrial tribunal), to be awarded any payment by way of arrears of remuneration or damages in respect of a time earlier than two years before the date on which the proceedings were instituted.

2A. (1) Where on a complaint or reference made to an industrial tribunal under section 2 above, a dispute arises as to whether any work is of equal value as mentioned in section 1(2)(c) above the tribunal shall not determine that question unless

(a) it is satisfied that there are no reasonable grounds for determining that the work is of equal value as so mentioned; or

(b) it has required a member of the panel of independent experts to prepare a report with respect to that question and has received that report.

(2) Without prejudice to the generality of paragraph (a) of subsection (1) above, there shall be taken, for the purposes of that paragraph, to be no reasonable grounds for determining that the work of a woman is of equal value as mentioned in section 1(2)(c) above if—

(a) that work and the work of the man in question have been given different values on a study such as is mentioned in section 1(5) above; and

(b) there are no reasonable grounds for determining that the evaluation contained in the study was (within the meaning of subsection (3) below) made on a system which discriminates on grounds of sex.

(3) An evaluation contained in a study such as is mentioned in section 1(5) above is made on a system which discriminates on grounds of sex where a difference, or coincidence, between values set by that system on different demands under the same or different headings is not justifiable irrespective of the sex of the person on whom those demands are made.

(4) In paragraph (b) of subsection (1) above the reference to a member of the panel of independent experts is a reference to a person who is for the time being designated by the Advisory, Conciliation and Arbitration Service for the purposes of that paragraph as such a member, being neither a member of the Council of that Service nor one of its officers or servants.

Appendix III: The Industrial Tribunals (Rules of Procedure) (Equal Value Amendment) Regulations 1983 – S.I. 1983 No. 1807

The Secretary of State, in exercise of the powers conferred on him by paragraph 1 of Schedule 9 to the Employment Protection (Consolidation) Act 1978 and after consultation with the Council on Tribunals, hereby makes the following Regulations:—

Citation and commencement

1. These Regulations may be cited as the Industrial Tribunals (Rules of Procedure) (Equal Value Amendment) Regulations 1983 and shall come into operation on 1st January 1984.

Interpretation

2. In these Regulations—

"the Equal Pay Act" means the Equal Pay Act 1970, as amended, with particular reference to the amendments made by the Equal Pay (Amendment) Regulations 1983;

"the principal Regulations (England and Wales)" means the Industrial Tribunals (Rules of Procedure) Regulations 1980;

"the principal Regulations (Scotland)" means the Industrial Tribunals (Rules of Procedure) (Scotland) Regulations 1980;

"the principal Rules of Procedure (England and Wales)" means the Industrial Tribunals Rules of Procedure 1980 contained in Schedule 1 to the principal Regulations (England and Wales);

"the principal Rules of Procedure (Scotland)" means the Industrial Tribunals Rules of Procedure (Scotland) 1980 contained in Schedule 1 to the principal Regulations (Scotland)

and, unless the context otherwise requires, any expression to which a meaning has been assigned by Regulation 2 of the principal Regulations (England and Wales), or, as the case may be, of the principal Regulations (Scotland), shall have that meaning.

Proceedings of tribunals in cases involving equal value claims

3. In any proceedings before a tribunal involving a claim by an applicant which rests upon entitlement to the benefit of an equality clause by virtue of the operation of section 1(2)(*c*) of the Equal Pay Act—

(*a*) in a case in which the principal Regulations (England and Wales) have effect—

(i) those Regulations shall have effect in relation to that claim subject to the amendments contained in Part I of the Schedule to these Regulations; and

(ii) the principal Rules of Procedure (England and Wales) shall have effect in relation to the claim subject to the amendments contained in Part II of the Schedule to these Regulations except in so far as such amendments are expressed to apply only to the principal Rules of Procedure (Scotland); and

(*b*) in a case in which the principal Regulations (Scotland) have effect—

(i) those Regulations shall have effect in relation to that claim subject to the amendments contained in Part I of the Schedule to these Regulations; and

(ii) the principal Rules of Procedure (Scotland) shall have effect in relation to the claim subject to the amendments contained in Part II of the Schedule to these Regulations except in so far as such amendments are expressed to apply only to the principal Rules of Procedure (England and Wales).

SCHEDULE

Regulation 3

PART I

AMENDMENTS TO THE PRINCIPAL REGULATIONS (ENGLAND AND WALES) AND TO THE PRINCIPAL REGULATIONS (SCOTLAND)

1. In Regulation 2 (interpretation)—

(*a*) after the definition of "decision" there shall be inserted—

""the Equal Pay Act" means the Equal Pay Act 1970, as amended, with particular reference to the amendments made by the Equal Pay (Amendment) Regulations 1983;

"equal value claim" means a claim by an applicant which rests upon entitlement to the benefit of an equality clause by virtue of the operation of section 1(2)(*c*) of the Equal Pay Act;

"expert" means a member of the panel of independent experts within the meaning of section 2A(4) of the Equal Pay Act;" and

(*b*) after the definition of "Register" there shall be inserted—
"“report" means a report required by a tribunal to be prepared by an expert, pursuant to section 2A(1)(*b*) of the Equal Pay Act;".

PART II

AMENDMENTS TO THE PRINCIPAL RULES OF PROCEDURE (ENGLAND AND WALES) AND TO THE PRINCIPAL RULES OF PROCEDURE (SCOTLAND)

1.—(1) In Rule 4, after paragraph (1), there shall be inserted—

"(1A) Subject to paragraph (1B), in a case involving an equal value claim, a tribunal may, on the application of an expert who has been required by the tribunal to prepare a report,—

(*a*) require any person who the tribunal is satisfied may have information which may be relevant to the question or matter on which the expert is required to report to furnish, in writing, such information as the tribunal may require;

(*b*) require any person to produce any documents which are in the possession, custody or power of that person and which the tribunal is satisfied may contain matter relevant to the question on which the expert is required to report;

and any information so required to be furnished or document so required to be produced shall be furnished or produced, at or within such time as the tribunal may appoint, to the Secretary of the Tribunals who shall send the information or document to the expert.

(1B) A tribunal shall not make a requirement under paragraph (1A) of this Rule—

(*a*) of a conciliation officer who has acted in connection with the complaint under section 64 of the Sex Discrimination Act 1975, or

(*b*) if it is satisfied that the person so required would have good grounds for refusing to comply with the requirement if it were a requirement made in connection with a hearing before the tribunal."

(2) In Rule 4, after paragraph (2), there shall be inserted—

"(2A) A person, whether or not a party to the proceedings,

upon whom a requirement has been made under paragraph (1A) of this Rule, may apply to the tribunal by notice to the Secretary of the Tribunals before the appointed time at or within which the requirement is to be complied with to vary or set aside the requirement. Notice of such application shall be given to the parties and to the expert upon whose application the requirement was made.".

(3) In paragraph (3) of Rule 4, after the words "(1)(iii)", there shall be inserted the words, "or paragraph (1A)".

2. After Rule 7, there shall be inserted—

"7A.—(1) In any case involving an equal value claim where a dispute arises as to whether any work is of equal value to other work in terms of the demands made on the person employed on the work (for instance under such headings as effort, skill and decision) (in this Rule hereinafter referred to as "the question"), a tribunal shall, before considering the question, except in cases to which Section 2A (1)(*a*) of the Equal Pay Act applies, require an expert to prepare a report with respect to the question: and the requirement shall be made in accordance with paragraphs (2) and (3) of this Rule.

(2) The requirement shall be made in writing and shall set out—

(*a*) the name and address of each of the parties;

(*b*) the address of the establishment at which the applicant is (or, as the case may be, was) employed;

(*c*) the question, and

(*d*) the identity of the person with reference to whose work the question arises

and a copy of the requirement shall be sent to each of the parties.

(3) The requirement shall stipulate that the expert shall—

(*a*) take account of all such information supplied and all such representations made to him as have a bearing on the question;

(*b*) before drawing up his report, produce and send to the parties a written summary of the said information and representations and invite the representations of the parties upon the material contained therein;

(*c*) make his report to the tribunal in a document which shall reproduce the summary and contain a brief account of any representations received from the parties upon it, any conclusion he may have reached upon the question and the reasons for that conclusion or, as the case may be, for his failure to reach such a conclusion;

(*d*) take no account of the difference of sex and at all times act fairly.

(4) Without prejudice to the generality of Rule 12(2)(*b*), where a tribunal requires an expert to prepare a report, it shall adjourn the hearing.

(5) If, on the application of one or more of the parties made not less than 42 days after a tribunal has notified an expert of the requirement to prepare a report, the tribunal forms the view that there has been or is likely to be undue delay in receiving that report, the tribunal may require the expert to provide in writing to the tribunal an explanation for the delay or information as to his progress and may, on consideration of any such explanation or information as may be provided and after seeking representations from the parties, revoke, by notice in writing to the expert, the requirement to prepare a report; and in such a case paragraph (1) of this Rule shall again apply.

(6) Where a tribunal has received the report of an expert, it shall forthwith send a copy of the report to each of the parties and shall fix a date for the hearing of the case to be resumed: provided that the date so fixed shall be at least 14 days after the date on which the report is sent to the parties.

(7) Upon the resuming of the hearing of the case in accordance with paragraph (6) of this Rule the report shall be admitted as evidence in the case unless the tribunal has exercised its power under paragraph (8) of this Rule not to admit the report.

(8) Where the tribunal, on the application of one or more of the parties or otherwise, forms the view–

(*a*) that the expert has not complied with a stipulation in paragraph (3) of this Rule, or

(*b*) that the conclusion contained in the report is one which, taking due account of the information supplied and representations made to the expert, could not reasonably have been reached, or

(*c*) that for some other material reason (other than disagreement with the conclusion that the applicant's work is or is not of equal value or with the reasoning leading to that conclusion) the report is unsatisfactory,

the tribunal may, if it thinks fit, determine not to admit the report; and in such a case paragraph (1) of this Rule shall again apply.

(9) In forming its view on the matters contained in paragraph (8)(*a*), (*b*) and (*c*) of this Rule, the tribunal shall take account of any representations of the parties thereon and may in that connection, subject to Rule 8(2A) and (2B), permit any party to give evidence upon, to call witnesses and to question any witness upon any matter relevant thereto.

(10) The tribunal may, at any time after it has received the report of an expert, require that expert (or, if that is impracticable, another expert) to explain any matter contained in his report or, having regard to such matters as may be set out in the requirement, to give further consideration to the question.

(11) The requirement in paragraph (10) of this Rule shall comply with paragraph (2) of this Rule and shall stipulate that the expert shall make his reply in writing to the tribunal, giving his explanation or, as the case may be, setting down any conclusion which may result from his further consideration and his reasons for that conclusion.

(12) Where the tribunal has received a reply from the expert under paragraph (11) of this Rule, it shall forthwith send a copy of the reply to each of the parties and shall allow the parties to make representations thereon; and the reply shall be treated as information furnished to the tribunal and be given such weight as the tribunal thinks fit.

(13) Where a tribunal has determined not to admit a report under paragraph (8), that report shall be treated for all purposes (other than the award of costs or expenses under Rule 11) connected with the proceedings as if it had not been received by the tribunal and no further account shall be taken of it; and the requirement on the expert to prepare a report shall lapse."

3.—(1) In paragraph (1) of Rule 8, at the beginning, there shall be inserted the words "Subject to paragraphs (2A), (2B), (2C), (2D) and (2E) of this Rule".

(2) In paragraph (2) of Rule 8, for the words "paragraph (1)", there shall be substituted the words "paragraphs (1), (2A), (2B), (2C) and (2D)".

(3) In Rule 8, after paragraph (2), there shall be inserted—

"(2A) The tribunal may, and shall upon the application of a party, require the attendance of an expert who has prepared a report in connection with an equal value claim in any hearing relating to that claim. Where an expert attends in compliance with such requirement any party may, subject to paragraph (1) of this Rule, cross-examine the expert on his report and on any other matter pertaining to the question on which the expert was required to report.

(2B) In a case involving an equal value claim, at any time after the tribunal has received the report of the expert, any party may, on giving reasonable notice of his intention to do so to the tribunal and to any other party to the claim, call one witness to give expert evidence on the question on which the tribunal has required the expert to prepare a report; and where such evidence is given, any other party may cross-examine the person giving that evidence upon it.

(2C) Except as provided in Rule 7A(9) or by paragraph (2D) of this Rule, no party to a case involving an equal value claim may give evidence upon, or question any witness upon, any matter of fact upon which a conclusion in the report of the expert is based.

(2D) Subject to paragraphs (2A) and (2B) of this Rule, a tribunal may, notwithstanding paragraph (2C) of this Rule, permit a party to give evidence upon, to call witnesses and to question any witness upon any such matters of fact as are referred to in that paragraph if either—

(a) the matter of fact is relevant to and is raised in connection with the issue contained in subsection (3) of section 1 of the Equal Pay Act (defence of genuine material factor) upon which the determination of the tribunal is being sought; or

(b) the report of the expert contains no conclusion on the question of whether the applicant's work and the work of the person identified in the requirement of the tribunal under Rule 7A(2) are of equal value and the tribunal is satisfied that the absence of that conclusion is wholly or mainly due to the refusal or deliberate omission of a person required by the tribunal under Rule 4(1A) to furnish information or to produce documents to comply with that requirement.

(2E) In a case involving an equal value claim, a tribunal may, on the application of a party, if in the circumstances of the case, having regard to the considerations expressed in paragraph (1) of this Rule, it considers that it is appropriate so to proceed, hear evidence upon and permit the parties to address it upon the issue contained in subsection (3) of section 1 of the Equal Pay Act (defence of genuine material factor) before it requires an expert to prepare a report under Rule 7A. Where the tribunal so proceeds, it shall be without prejudice to further consideration of that issue after the tribunal has received the report.".

4.—(1) In paragraph (2) of Rule 9, at the end, there shall be inserted the words "and in a case involving an equal value claim there shall be appended to that document a copy of the report (if any) of an expert received by the tribunal in the course of the proceedings.".

(2) In paragraph (3) of Rule 9, after the words "the chairman" there shall be inserted the words "and any report appended to the document pursuant to paragraph (2) of this Rule", and for the word "it" there shall be substituted the word "them".

(3) In Rule 9 of the principal Rules of Procedure (England and Wales), after paragraph (4), there shall be inserted—

"(4A) In any case involving an equal value claim where evidence has been heard in private, any matter bearing upon the substance of that evidence contained in any report of an expert may, if the tribunal so directs, be omitted from the report appended to the document pursuant to paragraph (2) of this Rule, and in that event a copy of the report without that omission shall be sent to any superior court in any proceedings relating to the decision on the case, together with a copy of the entry.".

(4) In Rule 9 of the principal Rules of Procedure (Scotland), after paragraph (4), there shall be inserted—

"(4A) In any case involving an equal value claim where evidence has been heard in private, any matter bearing upon the substance of that evidence contained in any report of an expert may, if the tribunal so directs, be omitted from the report appended to the document pursuant to paragraph (2) of this Rule, and in that event a copy of the report without that omission shall be sent to any appellate court in any proceedings relating to the decision on the case, together with a copy of the entry.".

5.—(1) In paragraph (1)(*b*) of Rule 11, after the word "tribunals" there shall be inserted the word ", experts".

(2) In Rule 11 of the principal Rules of Procedure (England and Wales), after paragraph (1), there shall be inserted—

"(1A) For the purposes of paragraph (1)(*a*) of this Rule, in a case involving an equal value claim, the costs or expenses in respect of which a tribunal may make an order include costs or expenses incurred by the party in whose favour the order is to be made in or in connection with the investigations carried out by the expert in preparing his report.".

(3) In Rule 11 of the principal Rules of Procedure (Scotland), after paragraph (1), there shall be inserted—

"(1A) For the purposes of paragraph (1)(*a*) of this Rule, in a case involving an equal value claim, the expenses in respect of which a tribunal may make an order include expenses incurred by the party in whose favour the order is to be made in or in connection with the investigations carried out by the expert in preparing his report.".

6.—(1) In Rule 12, after paragraph (2) there shall be inserted—

"(2A) Without prejudice to the generality of paragraph (2)(*b*) of this Rule, in a case involving an equal value claim the tribunal shall, before proceeding to hear the parties on the claim, invite them to apply for an adjournment for the purpose of seeking to reach a settlement of the claim and shall, if both or all the parties agree to such a course, grant an adjournment for that purpose.

(2B) If, in a case involving an equal value claim, after the tribunal has adjourned the hearing under rule 7A(4) but before the tribunal has received the report of the expert, the applicant gives notice under paragraph (2)(*c*) of this Rule, the tribunal shall forthwith notify the expert that the requirement to prepare a report has ceased. The notice shall be without prejudice to the operation of Rule 11(1A).".

(2) In paragraph (3) of Rule 12, after the words "Rule 4(2)" there shall be inserted the words "and (2A)", after the words "Secretary of State"

there shall be inserted the words "or, in the case of an application under Rule 4(1A), the expert" and after the word "parties", there shall be inserted the words "(or, in the case of an application by an expert, the parties and any other person in respect of whom the tribunal is asked, in the application, to impose a requirement)".

7.—(1) In paragraph (4) of Rule 17, after the words "conciliation officer" there shall be inserted the words "and the appropriate expert".

(2) In paragraph (5)(*b*) of Rule 17, after the words "Rule 4(1)(iii)" there shall be inserted the words "or (1A)".

(3) In paragraph (9) of Rule 17, the words '1970(a)" and the footnote pertaining thereto shall be deleted.

Appendix IV: List of Cases

Appendix V: Table of Statutes

Addendum: Discriminatory Job Evaluation

As the proofs of this book were being corrected, the transcript of the first Industrial Tribunal decision under the Regulations, *Neil and Others v. Ford Motor Co. Ltd*, became available. Examination of this decision shows that, if anything, in my analysis of the sections of the Regulations dealing with discriminatory job evaluation, I underestimated the complexities posed by the language used in s.A(2)(b) and s.2A(3).

This case concerned a claim by female sewing machinists that their work is of equal value to the work of three groups of men placed in a higher grade under the company's evaluation scheme. The Industrial Tribunal hearing on whether the claim was blocked by s.2A(2)(b) and s.2A(3) lasted six days and resulted in a 29-page decision.

The argument on behalf of the applicants was that s.2A(2)(a) merely required the Tribunal to be satisfied that the applicant's case was reasonably arguable and that under s.2A(3) it was sufficient that the Tribunal conclude that it was reasonably arguable that the evaluation was not 'justifiable' in the sense that it was 'wrong'. It was contended that there was no further requirement to show that the cause of the wrong valuation was sex discrimination. In the alternative, it was contended that there was evidence from which it could be inferred that the job evaluation in this case was tainted by sex discrimination.

The Industrial Tribunal, by a majority decision, concluded:

> There is . . . no presumption that a job evaluation study is one that discriminates on grounds of sex, and in the absence of a presumption it is difficult to accept that the burden of proof can lie on the respondents to a claim. Nor can the majority of us accept the proposition that the applicants have only to put forward a reasonable argument which is not foredoomed to failure. If an argument is reasonable it still may not prevail against other reasonable arguments, but it should not be foredoomed to failure; if it is so foredoomed, it is unlikely to be reasonable. We appreciate that a Tribunal should not be reluctant to draw inferences, where there are reasonable grounds for drawing them, but we are not simply engaged in something equivalent to a pre-hearing assessment and we should not lightly set in train a new evaluation unless we are tolerably certain that there are reasonable grounds for believing

> the previous job evaluation study to have been distorted by discrimination.

On that basis, the Tribunal majority directed itself that:

> what in effect section 2A(2) and (3) require us to ask ourselves in the present case is whether there is any good reason to suppose that any one or more of the demands, or characteristics on which values have been set by the system, ought in fairness to have been given a value more favourable to the applicant and would have been given such a value, if the majority of those from whose assessments the values were derived had not consciously or subconsciously been influenced by consideration of the sex of those on whom the demands would chiefly be made. There would be a sufficient reason for such a supposition, if we found that a traditionally female attribute or skill was undervalued or any traditionally male attribute was overvalued.

The majority of the Tribunal went on to find that there was 'no sufficient reason to persuade us that any comparative value set by the system on any demand or characteristic was unfavourable to women or was the consequence of any conscious or unconscious sexual bias or prejudice'.

The Tribunal's decision in this case accords in general terms with the view I have taken in Chapter 6 that a standard of discrimination must be read into s.2A(3). As that chapter makes clear, however, it is doubtful whether it is correct to define discrimination in terms of 'conscious or unconscious sexual bias'. Such a definition, it may be contended, fails to give full effect to the concept of indirect discrimination – which is concerned only with impact and not with motive. The discrimination issue is not restricted to the undervaluation of traditionally female attributes; it also encompasses the unjustifiable overvaluation of a neutral attribute – such as working conditions – which has an adverse impact on the particular women making the claim in comparison with their male comparators.

The *Ford* decision also starkly highlights the additional confusion which stems from the 'no reasonable grounds' standard in s.2A(2), a point which requires additional treatment to that accorded to it in Chapter 6. Given that what must be shown is that the job evaluation scheme has discriminated, the standard of proof, in theory, could range from a mere requirement to show an arguable case to a requirement to satisfy the Tribunal on the balance of probabilities that the system was sexually discriminatory. Without ever saying so in terms, the Industrial Tribunal in this case plumps for a convincing showing of discrimination on the evidence. But the difficulty in construction is that the higher the standard of proof required, the less effect is given to the use of the phrase 'no reasonable grounds'. As we pointed out in Chapter 6, the relevant provision would make equal sense without that phrase; then the Industrial Tribunal would be required simply to determine whether 'the evaluation contained in the study . . . was made on a system which discriminates on grounds of sex'.

On normal principles of construction, the additional words 'no reasonable grounds' must serve some purpose, yet, if anything less than the ordinary burden of proof is contemplated, it is difficult to see how it can operate satisfactorily in practice. There is no reason for believing that the draftsman contemplated any evidential restrictions in this context (unlike, for example, an interlocutory injunction where an order may be made on the basis of a good arguable case based on affidavit evidence only on the reasoning that further evidence will emerge at the trial of the action). Given that, any evidence of an arguable case or a prima facie case of discrimination can be rebutted by evidence from the employer. Moreover, once it is accepted that what must be shown is that there has been sex discrimination, on policy grounds it is important that the employer be given a full opportunity to refute any allegation of discriminatory behaviour.

In this sense, the respective interpretations of s.2A(2) and s.2A(3) stand or fall together. If the Tribunal does not have to find any discrimination and can allow the claim through simply because it believes the outcome of the job evaluation may have been wrong, it may be thought sufficient that an arguable case has been made. Of course, such a construction would fail to give effect to the express criterion in the statute that whether the claim can proceed depends on whether there has been sex discrimination. If, on the other hand, the Tribunal must decide whether the employer has discriminated, such a determination should be made on the ordinary standards of proof. My own view is that the latter construction is preferable, notwithstanding that it necessitates giving little weight to the phrase 'no reasonable grounds'.

July 1984 MICHAEL RUBENSTEIN

Bibliography

The literature on the problems addressed in this book is vast. The economics of discrimination is a burgeoning field for research, particularly in the United States. American legal commentary is also helpful for understanding the British Regulations. In *County of Washington* v. *Gunther*, the Supreme Court held that pay discrimination claims could be brought under US discrimination law even if the work being compared did not fall within the standard of equality under the American Equal Pay Act. Since then, 'comparable worth' – the American phrase approximating to 'equal pay for work of equal value' – has been regarded as the discrimination issue for the 1980s. Although there are important differences between the relevant statutes in the two countries, the underlying similarities between British and American discrimination law are such that similar issues are raised. In this bibliography, therefore, I have included some of the more interesting American legal commentaries. For a relatively comprehensive list of American sources on equal pay law, I would ask the reader to await my comparative study of equal pay law generally in Britain and America, still in the course of preparation.

The most useful British analyses of the new Regulations and their implications are also listed below. I have not included references to Parliamentary Debates or to some other official documents, but these will be found in the relevant footnotes to the text.

C. Aldred, *Women at Work* (London: Pan Books, 1981).

A. H. Amsden (ed) *The Economics of Women and Work* (Harmondsworth: Penguin Books, 1980).

S. Atkins, 'Equal Pay for Work of Equal Value', *Public Law*, Spring, 1983.

B. A. Babcock, A. E. Freedman, E. H. Norton and S. C. Ross, *Sex Discrimination and the Law: Causes and Remedies* (Boston: Little, Brown and Co, 1975).

E. Barnett, 'Comparable Worth and the Equal Pay Act – Proving Sex-Based Wage Discrimination Claims After County of Washington v. Gunther', *Wayne Law Review*, vol. 28:1669, 1982.

J. R. Bellace, *Equal Pay for Work of Equal Value: The Impact of the Legal Mandate on Job Evaluation*, Paper presented at the 20th Congress of Applied Psychology, Edinburgh, July, 1982.

A. H. Beller, 'Title VII and the Male/Female Earnings Gap: An Economic Analysis', *Harvard Women's Law Journal*, vol. 1, no. 1, Spring, 1978.

F. D. Blau, *Equal Pay in the Office* (Farnborough: Lexington Books, 1977).

M. Blaxall and B. Reagan (eds) *Women and the Workplace: The Implications of Occupational Segregation* (Chicago and London: University of Chicago Press, 1976).

R. G. Blumrosen, 'Wage Discrimination, Job Segregation, and Title VII of the Civil Rights Act of 1964', *University of Michigan Journal of Law Reform*, vol. 12: 397, 1979.

R. G. Blumrosen, 'Wage Discrimination and Job Segregation: The Survival of a Theory', *University of Michigan Journal of Law Reform*, vol. 14:1, 1980.

G. L. Buckingham, *What to do about Equal Pay for Women* (Epping: Gower Press, 1973).

Bureau of National Affairs, *The Comparable Worth Issue: A BNA Special Report* (Washington, 1981).

Central Arbitration Committee, *Annual Report*, 1977.

J. R. Chapman (ed) *Economic Independence for Women: The Foundation for Equal Rights* (Beverly Hills and London: Sage Publications, 1976).

B. Chiplin and P. J. Sloane, *Sex Discrimination in the Labour Market* (London: Macmillan, 1976).

B. Chiplin and P. J. Sloane, *Tackling Discrimination at the Workplace: An Analysis of Sex Discrimination in Britain* (Cambridge University Press, 1982).

L. Clarke, 'Proposed Amendments to the Equal Pay Act 1970', *New Law Journal*, 21 October, 1983 and 23 December, 1983.

L. Clarke, 'Equal Pay for Work of Equal Value', *New Law Journal*, 24 February, 1984.

'Comparable Worth', *ILR Report*, vol. XIX, no. 2, Spring, 1982.

M. Corcoran and G. J. Duncan, 'Work history, labor force attachment, and earnings differences between the races and sexes', *Journal of Human Resources*, vol. 14:3, Winter, 1979.

J. Coussins, *The Equality Report* (London: National Council for Civil Liberties, 1976).

W. B. Creighton, *Working Women and the Law* (London: Mansell, 1979).

P. L. Davies, 'The Central Arbitration Committee and Equal Pay', *Current Legal Problems*, 1980.

R. Davies, *Women and Work* (London: Arrow Books, 1975).

Department of Employment, *Women & Work: a statistical survey*, DE Manpower Paper No. 9 (London: HMSO, 1974).

Department of Employment, *Women & Work: Sex Differences and Society*, DE Manpower Paper No. 10 (London: HMSO, 1974).

Department of Employment, *Women & Work: a review*, DE Manpower Paper No. 11 (London: HMSO, 1975).

P. B. Doeringer, 'Determinants of the Structure of Industrial-Type Labor Markets', *Industrial and Labor Relations Review*, vol. 20:206, January, 1967.

P. B. Doeringer and M. J. Piore, *Internal Labor Markets and Manpower Analysis*, D. C. Heath & Co, 1971.

EEOC, Hearings before *The United States Equal Employment Opportunity*

Commisssion on Job Segregation and Wage Discrimination, 28–30 April, 1980.

Equal Opportunities Commission, *Annual Reports*, HMSO.

Equal Opportunities Commission, *EOC Research Bulletin*, vol. 1, no. 1, Winter, 1978–9.

Equal Opportunities Commission, *Women and Underachievement at Work*, EOC Research Bulletin No. 5, Spring, 1981.

Equal Opportunities Commission, *Job Evaluation Schemes Free of Sex Bias*.

Equal Opportunities Commission, *Response to the Draft Order to Amend The Equal Pay Act 1970*, 28 February, 1983.

Equal Opportunities Commission, *Leading Counsel's Opinion on the Proposed Amendments to The Equal Pay Act 1970*, March, 1983.

'Equal Pay, Comparable Work, and Job Evaluation', *Yale Law Journal*, vol. 90:633, 1981.

'Equal Pay for Comparable Work', *Harvard Civil Rights–Civil Liberties Law Review*, vol. 15:475, 1980.

K. D. Ewing, 'Equal Pay For Work Of Equal Value', *The Scots Law Times*, 27 May, 1983.

Fawcett Society, *Report on a Conference on Equal Pay for Work of Equal Value*, 12 February, 1983.

G. T. Floros, 'Comparable Worth Theory of Title VII Sex Discrimination In Compensation', *Missouri Law Review*, vol. 47:495, 1982.

L. N. Gasaway, 'Comparable Worth: A Post-Gunther Overview', *The Georgetown Law Journal*, vol. 69:1123, 1981.

M. G. Gatlin, 'Increasing Protection for Women in the Area of Gender-Based Wage Discrimination', *New England Law Review*, vol. 17:2, 1982.

General Household Survey 1980, HMSO.

T. Gill and L. Whitty, *Women's Rights in the Workplace* (Harmondsworth: Penguin Books, 1983).

P. Glucklich, M. Povall, M. W. Snell and A. Zell, 'Equal pay and opportunity', *Department of Employment Gazette*, July, 1978.

M. E. Gold, *A Dialogue on Comparable Worth* (Ithaca: ILR Press, 1983).

R. Greaves, 'Article 119 and its Interpretation by the European Court of Justice', Northern Ireland Legal Quarterly, vol. 33:3, Autumn, 1982.

D. L. Gregory, 'Comparable Worth: The Demise of the Disparate Impact Theory of Liability', *Detroit College of Law Review*, vol. IV:853, 1982.

J. A. Grune (ed) *Manual on Pay Equity: Raising Wages for Women's Work*, Conference on Alternative State and Local Policies, Committee on Pay Equity, Washington, 1980.

C. Hakim, *Occupational Segregation: A comparative study of the degree and pattern of the differentiation between men and women's work in Britain, the United States and other countries*, Department of Employment, Research Paper No. 9, November, 1979.

A. Hartman, 'Comparable Worth', *Harvard Women's Law Journal*, vol. 6:1, Spring, 1983.

K. J. Headley, 'Title VII Comparable Worth Claims', *San Diego Law Review*, vol. 18:685, July, 1981.

J. Hebden, 'Men's and Women's Pay in Britain', *Industrial Relations Journal*, vol. 9:2, Summer, 1978.

M. S. Helmreich, 'Women, Wages and Title VII: The Significance of County of Washington v. Gunther', *University of Pittsburgh Law Review*, vol. 43:467, 1982.

A. Hunt, *A Survey of Women's Employment* (London: HMSO, 1968).

A. Hunt, *Management Attitudes and Practices towards Women at Work: An employment policy survey carried out on behalf of the Department of Employment* (London: HMSO, 1975).

International Labour Office, *Women workers and society*, Geneva, 1976.

H. C. Jain and P. J. Sloane, 'Race, Sex and Minority Group Discrimination Legislation in North America and Britain', *Industrial Relations Journal*, vol. 9:2, Summer, 1978.

H. C. Jain and P. J. Sloane, *Equal Employment Issues: Race and Sex Discrimination in the United States, Canada, and Britain* (New York: Praeger: 1981).

L. Kanowitz, *Women and The Law: The Unfinished Revolution* (Albuquerque: University of New Mexico Press, 1969).

B. Lang, 'The New Equal Pay Regulations', *Legal Action*, March, 1984.

C. A. Larsen, 'Equal Pay for Women in the United Kingdom', *International Labour Review*, vol. 103:1, January, 1971.

A. Larson, *Employment Discrimination* (New York: Matthew Bender, 1978).

R. Layard *et al.*, *The Causes of Poverty*, Background Paper No. 5, Royal Commission on the Distribution of Income & Wealth, HMSO, 1978.

A. Lester, 'Unequal Pay – Unequal Justice', *New Law Journal*, 28 October, 1983.

A. Lester and D. Wainwright, *Equal Pay for Work of Equal Value: Law and Practice* (London: TMS Management Consultants, 1984).

C. S. Licata, 'Beyond The Bennett Amendment: Establishing A Prima Facie Case of Sexual Discrimination in Compensation Under Title VII', *St John's Law Review*, vol. 54:738, 1980.

E. R. Livernash (ed) *Comparable Worth: Issues and Alternatives* (Washington: Equal Employment Advisory Council, 1980).

C. B. Lloyd and B. T. Niemi, *The Economics of Sex Differentials* (New York: Columbia University Press, 1979).

J. P. Lowry, 'Equal Pay for Work of Equal Value: How the New Regulations Will Work', *Personnel Management*, September, 1983.

L. Lustgarten, *Legal Control of Racial Discrimination* (London: Macmillan, 1980).

C. A. MacKinnon, *Sexual Harassment of Working Women* (New Haven and London: Yale University Press, 1979).

J. F. Madden, 'Economic Rational for Sex Differences in Education', *Southern Economic Review*, April 1978.

M. Malone, *A Practical Guide to Discrimination Law* (London: Grant McIntyre, 1980).

C. McCrudden, 'Equal Pay for Work of Equal Value: the Equal Pay (Amendment) Regulations 1983', *The Industrial Law Journal*, vol. 12:4 December, 1983.

C. McCrudden, 'Equal Pay for Work of Equal Value', *The Industrial Law Journal*, vol. 13:1, March, 1984.

J. Mincer and S. Polachek, 'Family Investments in Human Capital', *Journal of Political Economy*, vol. 82:76, March–April 1974.

B. W. Napier, 'Equal Pay for Work of Equal Value', *The Scots Law Times*, 10 February, 1984.

National Board for Prices and Incomes, *General Problems of Low Pay*, Report No. 169, Cmnd 4648, HMSO, April, 1971.

B. A. Nelson, E. M. Opton and T. E. Wilson, 'Wage Discrimination and the "Comparable Worth" Theory in Perspective', *University of Michigan Journal of Law Reform*, vol. 13:233, Winter, 1980.

W. Newman and J. Vonhof, '"Separate But Equal" – Job Segregation and Pay Equity in the Wake of Gunther', *University of Illinois Law Review*, 1981: 271.

B. A. Norris, 'Comparable Worth, Disparate Impact, and the Market Rate Salary Problem: A Legal Analysis and Statistical Application', *California Law Review*, vol. 71:730, 1983.

V. Novarra, *Women's Work, Men's Work: The Ambivalence of Equality* (London: Marion Boyars, 1980).

Office of Manpower Economics, *Equal Pay* (London: HMSO, 1972).

J. O'Neil, 'The "Comparable Worth" Trap', *The Wall Street Journal*, 23 January, 1984.

P. Paterson and M. Armstrong, *An Employer's Guide to Equal Pay* (London: Kogan Page (Associates), 1972).

Pay Equity: Equal Pay for Work of Comparable Value, Joint Hearings before the Subcommittees on Human Resources, Civil Service, Compensation and Employee Benefits of the Committee on Post Office and Civil Service, House of Representatives, 97th Congress (Washington: US Government Printing Office, 1983).

B. Pettman (ed) *Equal Pay for Women: Progress and Problems in Seven Countries* (Bradford: MCB Books, 1975).

E. S. Phelps, 'The Statistical Theory of Racism and Sexism', *American Economic Review*, vol. 62:659, September, 1972.

H. Phelps Brown, *The Inequality of Pay* (Oxford University Press, 1977).

S. Polachek, 'Occupational Segregation: An Alternative Hypothesis', *Journal of Contemporary Business*, Winter, 1976.

R. S. Ratner (ed) *Equal Employment Policy For Women: Strategies for Implementation in the United States, Canada, and Western Europe* (Philadelphia: Temple University Press, 1980).

I. Reid and E. Wormald (eds) *Sex Differences in Britain* (London: Grant McIntyre, 1982).

Rights of Women Europe, *Women's Rights & The EEC: A Guide for Women in the UK*, London, 1983.

Royal Commission on the Distribution of Income & Wealth, Report No. 6, *Lower Incomes* (London: HMSO, 1978).

Royal Commission on the Distribution of Income & Wealth, *Selected Evidence*, Report No. 6 (London: HMSO, 1978).

M. Rubenstein, 'The Law of Sexual Harassment at Work, *The Industrial Law Journal*, vol. 12:1, March, 1983.

M. Rubenstein, 'Discriminatory Job Evaluation Schemes and the Equal Pay (Amendment) Regulations, *New Law Journal*, 18 November, 1983.

B. L. Schlei and P. Grossman, *Employment Discrimination Law*, 2nd ed. (Washington: The Bureau of National Affairs, 1983).

F. Schmidt (ed) *Discrimination in Employment: A Study of Six Countries by the Comparative Labour Law Group* (Stockholm: Almqvist & Wiksell International, 1978).

P. G. Schofield, 'Equal Pay for Work of Equal Value: Commission of the European Communities v. UK', *The Industrial Law Journal*, vol. 11: 4, December, 1982.

M. B. Seidenfeld, 'Sex-Based Wage Discrimination Under The Title VII Disparate Impact Doctrine', *Stanford Law Review*, vol. 34:1083, May, 1982.

L. L. Shapiro, 'Sex-Based Wage Discrimination: One Step Beyond The Equal Pay Act', *Hofstra Law Review*, vol. 9:1526, 1981.

P. J. Sloane (ed) *Women and Low Pay* (London: Macmillan, 1980).

P. J. Sloane, *The Earnings Gap Between Men and Women in Britain* (London: Social Science Research Council, 1981).

M. W. Snell, P. Glucklich and M. Povall, *Equal Pay and Opportunities: A Study of the Implementation and Effects of the Equal Pay and Sex Discrimination Acts in 26 Organisations*, Department of Employment, Research Paper No. 20, April, 1981.

'Staff job evaluation', *Industrial Relations Review & Report*, No. 310, 20 December, 1983.

C. A. Sullivan, M. J. Zimmer and R. F. Richards, *Federal Statutory Law of Employment Discrimination* (Indianapolis: The Michie Co/Bobbs-Merrill, 1980).

E. Szyszczak, 'Differences in Pay for Part-time Work', *The Modern Law Review*, vol. 44:6, November, 1981.

'The New Equal Pay Law', *Industrial Relations Legal Information Bulletin*, No. 249, 24 January, 1984.

Thirteenth Report from the Joint Committee on Statutory Instruments, Session 1983–4, HMSO.

R. Townshend-Smith, 'The Equal Pay (Amendment) Regulations 1983, *The Modern Law Review*, vol. 47:2, March, 1984.

Trade Union Research Unit, *Women and Job Evaluation: The Implications of the Proposed Amendment to the Equal Pay Act*, Discussion Paper No. 29, March, 1983.

D. J. Treiman and H. I. Hartmann (eds) *Women, Work, and Wages: Equal Pay for Jobs of Equal Value* (Washington: National Academy Press, 1981).

United States Department of Labor, *The Earnings Gap Between Women and Men*, Washington, 1976.

P. A. Wallace and A. M. LaMond, *Women, Minorities, and Employment Discrimination* (Lexington: Lexington Books, 1977).

A. Weir and M. McIntosh, 'Towards a Wages Strategy for Women', *Feminist Review*, vol. 10, Spring, 1982.

Index